Managing International Business in Relation-Based versus Rule-Based Countries

Managing International Business in Relation-Based versus Rule-Based Countries

Shaomin Li

First published in 2009 by
Business Expert Press, LLC
222 East 46th Street, New York, NY 10017
www.businessexpertpress.com

ISBN–13: 978–1–60649–084–6 (paperback)
ISBN–10: 1–60649–084–2 (paperback)

ISBN–13: 978–1–60649–085–3 (e-book)
ISBN–10: 1–60649–085–0 (e-book)

DOI 10.4128/9781606490853

A publication in the Business Expert Press International Business collection

Collection ISSN (print) 1948–2752
Collection ISSN (electronic) 1948–2760

Cover design by Artistic Group—Monroe, NY
Interior design by Scribe, Inc.

First edition: December 2009

10 9 8 7 6 5 4 3 2 1

Printed in the United States of America.

For my parents, Amy, and Diana

Abstract

This book summarizes the research in the past 10 years on how different governance environments at the national level affect business operations and management. Its primary audience includes executives who manage business across borders. Readers interested in international political economy and comparative culture may also find it intriguing.

A country's governance environment includes the political, economic, and social systems that facilitate or constrain the way firms and individuals govern their social exchanges and business activities. This book distinguishes and examines the two major governance environments in the world, the rule-based system (conventionally called the "Western way") and the relation-based system (the "Asian way"), and demonstrates that the Asian way does not come from cultural heritage, but rather it is a result of the particular stage of political and economic development in which public rules are not fair and effective. The author argues that contrary to the conventional view that dismisses the relation-based way as backward, it may be efficient under certain conditions. This book further shows that the success of the relation-based way is not primarily based on the family but on a more extended informal social network beyond the family.

This book discusses how business operations and investments are protected and managed under relation-based governance and demonstrates that some major management difficulties and investment failures in international business that were previously puzzling can now be clearly explained by the lack of understanding of the key features of relation-based governance. This book concludes with discussions on the transition from relation-based to rule-based governance that many relation-based countries are going through, the special challenges of the transition, and how businesses and societies may successfully navigate through such a transition.

Keywords

rule-based (rules-based, public ordering), relation-based (relations-based, relationship-based, private-ordering), family-based, governance environment, Governance Environment Index (GEI), transition, social network (informal network), trust, generalized trust, particularized trust, extended particularized trust, nuclear particularized trust

Author's Note

This book is a result of a research project that was started after the 1997 Asian financial crisis and has continued for the following 10 years or so. The East Asian economies for many years had enjoyed rapid growth that created the "Asian miracle." Such a remarkable performance has been attributed to the "Asian way," namely, family members working together without calculating how much each got paid, something called "dedicated capitalism." And then the 1997 financial crisis hit Asia. The Asian model seemed to be in trouble and relying on the family became "crony capitalism." My colleagues and I were not satisfied with such an inconsistent explanation and were searching for an answer. How could the feature that had been viewed as the cause of the miracle now be blamed for the crisis? In general, what are the most important factors that distinguish the Asian way of doing business from the rest of the world?

After years of searching, we finally narrowed down to what is perhaps the single most important factor that distinguishes the "Asian way" of doing business from the West: governance environment, which we divided into "rule-based" and "relation-based." The idea then caught on quickly and was featured in leading media such as the *Economist* and the *Wall Street Journal*, among others. The application of our framework goes beyond Asia. It is now widely recognized that these two distinctive ways of conducting business can help explain some major puzzles and hidden difficulties in doing business globally. This book summarizes the research findings in this stream and is written primarily for business executives and readers—both academic and nonacademic—who are interested in this topic.

I have benefited greatly from the exchanges with my colleagues and students, who provide me vital feedback and generous encouragement in seminars, classes, and during coffee breaks. I especially would like to thank Ilan Alon, Jean Boddewyn, Lan Cao, Jie Chen, Mike Dugan, Bill Judge, Hae Ryong Kim, T. P. Liang, Seung Ho (Sam) Park, John Pollock, David Selover, Weijian Shan, Rosalie Siegel, Mike Stein, Tom Weber, Harris Wu, Judy Wu, Jun Xia, Andy Yan, Kuang Yeh, Dongsheng Zhou, and Haiwen Zhou. I also want to thank publisher David Parker; editors

Tamer Cavusgil, Michael Czinkota, and Matt Myers; production liaison Cindy Durand; and production manager Danny Constantino for their guidance and help.

My deepest gratitude goes to my wife, Amy, who shoulders all the family responsibilities so that I can write without any constraints; our daughter Diana, whose witty, humorous (and occasionally sarcastic) comments are like a fresh breeze in the hot summer days of writing; and Otto, the family shih-tzu who always sits quietly beside me when I am writing, giving me moral support without too much criticism.

Contents

Chapter 1 Introduction: Rule-Based Versus Relation-Based Systems . . 1

Chapter 2 Distinguishing Rule-Based and Relation-Based Countries: How to Measure Governance Environment 19

Chapter 3 Market Structure in Relation-Based Societies 33

Chapter 4 How Much Do We Trust Disclosed Information?: Investment Protection in Relation-Based Markets. 53

Chapter 5 Mafia Boss or Modern Manager?: Management and Working Relationships in Relation-Based Firms 65

Chapter 6 Friction Between Information and Communication Technology and Relation-Based Governance 83

Chapter 7 "Efficiency-Enhancing" Corruption?: Corruption in Relation-Based Societies 95

Chapter 8 The Greatest Leap Forward: The Transition From Relation-Based to Rule-Based Governance 111

Notes. 129

References 135

Index 141

CHAPTER 1

Introduction

Rule-Based Versus Relation-Based Systems

After a daylong meeting in New York, we—a group of Chinese businesspeople—went to a restaurant to eat. It was fun. "Together or separate checks?" The waitress asked us when we were almost done. "Together!" Someone shouted, and then a war broke out between us over who should pay. But if you think that we were trying to get someone else to pay, then you are wrong. Each of us competed for the bill.[1]

Why do the Chinese always compete to pay while most Americans "go Dutch" when a group of people eat out? Does this mean that in general the Chinese are more generous than Americans? Similar puzzles abound. For example, why do strangers usually smile or nod at each other when they pass each other on streets in America while unrelated people don't acknowledge each other's existence when they pass each other through a narrow alley in China? Does this mean that Americans are friendlier than the Chinese?

What is the economic significance of all those differences? Are these differences due to culture? If they are, what is behind the culture? With rapid globalization and cultural interaction, will the Americans adopt the Chinese way, or vice versa? In general, how can we explain the differences between the East and West in social and economic interactions in their societies, and what do these differences mean when the East meets the West?

In search of answers to these puzzles, I have been studying different social systems for the past 10 years and, based on new findings by myself and others, have developed a theoretical perspective that can offer some not-so-obvious and yet consistent explanations to these puzzles. These solutions not only greatly satisfied my own intellectual curiosity but also helped others to understand these puzzles from a new perspective. During more than a decade of teaching international business, I have asked many of my students the above puzzles and have gotten all sorts of answers, ranging from a tautological explanation (e.g., "This is just how things are") to a totally ridiculous response (e.g., "Americans are dumb so that they greet everyone"). And most of the answers did not make logical and consistent sense. I would then offer them my simple but not-so-obvious answers that can consistently and logically explain the reasons behind these seemingly unrelated patterns, and I could see my bright students' eyes light up and they would exclaim, "Aha! Now I see it."

Their favorable reaction to my view on the patterns of social economic interactions across countries over the years eventually made me sit down and write this book, which is *not* a boring academic book (at least I try not to make it boring). This book is for people who have a broad interest in learning how societies differ in certain fundamental ways and for people who always want to identify systematic patterns in what appear to be random differences. More importantly, the book is also written for business executives who need to understand *the reasons behind different business practices across countries*. In an increasingly globalized marketplace, such understanding is vital in order to effectively and efficiently navigate through different business environments and successfully operate and manage international business.

Now, let's leave the "together or separate checks" and the "street encounter" puzzles for the time being and think about a more direct economic question: What made the "East Asian economic miracle" possible? The reader may wonder how such an economic question of considerable significance has anything to do with those puzzles. As I will show in the book, they are closely related.

What Made the "East Asian Economic Miracle"?

The "East Asian economic miracle" usually refers to the sustained rapid economic growth achieved by the East Asian countries, including Japan after World War II, Hong Kong, Singapore, South Korea, Taiwan between the 1960s and 1980s, and China from the late 1970s to the present. A common feature in the political economy[2] of these countries is that to various degrees they are (or have been) ruled by a government not subject to effective checks and balances and a legal system that lacks independence and is influenced by the ruler(s), undermining its ability to protect property rights. As a result of those shortcomings, these countries are characterized by a powerful state and a high level of corruption.

Thus the main puzzle about the "East Asia economic miracle" is how these countries achieve an economic miracle under political rule that seems detrimental to economic development.

A great deal of research and scholarship has been devoted to offering explanations of what made the "East Asian economic miracle" possible. Rich and expanding literature has been produced on this debate. A novice reader can easily be led into a jungle and get lost in the vast amount of articles and books offering complicated and often conflicting views. Here I attempt to offer a map to navigate in this jungle, and I provide a unique path for the reader to walk out of the jungle and see the puzzle differently.

Perhaps the best known theory to explain the "Asian miracle" is the political explanation. It has been argued that under a (benevolent) dictator or authoritarian ruler who is not too corrupt and is pro business, a country's economy can be more effectively and efficiently developed. While this argument seems to fit the political experience of some of the countries within the "Asian miracle" set, such as South Korea under the military dictator Park Chung Hee and Taiwan under the rule of Chiang Kai Shek and his son Chiang Chin Kuo, *it fails to explain what makes a dictator benevolent and not too corrupt.* For example, why is it that Park and the Chiangs were not interested in accumulating personal wealth, while their counterparts in the Philippines (Marcos) and Indonesia (Suharto) were busily transferring huge amounts of public funds into their Swiss bank accounts? In general, according to the study by Przeworski and associates, *the chance that a country will embark on a rapid economic development is the same under either dictatorship or democracy.*[3]

Another dominant view on the "East Asian economic miracle" is offered by the cultural theorists who try to explain the miracle from a cultural perspective.[4] According to the cultural view, Asian countries are able to achieve high economic growth despite poor political systems (e.g., lacking democracy and the rule of law) because of the deeply rooted Confucian values in their societies that emphasize long-term economic views (e.g., save today for greater consumption value tomorrow; study hard today for a greater payoff in the future) and reciprocity in interpersonal relationships (e.g., you give me one drop of water when I am in need, and I will return with a water fountain in the future when I am able). While attributing the "East Asian economic miracle" to the Confucian culture may help us to see the link between a strong work ethic and economic growth, it only provides a partial explanation because there are still important questions left unanswered by culture. Even scholars who believe that culture makes almost all the difference in economic development admit that culture alone cannot consistently predict how an economy will develop. For example, *China has had the Confucian tradition for about 2,000 years. Why hasn't its economic development always been positive? Why has it been on and off from time to time?* Moreover, this approach fails to answer what shapes a culture. How does culture interact with the political, legal, and economic institutions in a society to collectively affect economic development and business activities in the society?

Unsatisfied with either the authoritarianism argument or the cultural-deterministic view briefly described above, scholars of social sciences have been searching for more convincing answers from different perspectives. Increasingly, these efforts converge to one aspect that is very important for economic activities and yet has been overlooked by the mainstream scholars in addressing what made the "East Asian economic miracle": governance.

Governance can be defined as a mechanism people use to protect their interest in social and economic exchanges. For example, in a society with a fair, open, and effective legal system, people would resort to the courts or public arbitrations for a ruling if disputes arise. On the other hand, when the law is biased and judges are corrupt, then people may not choose the public rule as their means of settling disputes. Instead, they may look for a private way to solve it, which may include mediation or even violence (such as kidnapping). Interestingly, scholars observe that *what governance mechanism people or firms choose in a society is not entirely up to the individual or firm; it is primarily determined by the dominant governance environment of the society in which they live or conduct business.*

Governance environment refers to the set of political, legal, and social institutions that collectively facilitates or constrains the choice of governance mechanism the individual or firm has in a society. Scholars of social sciences have now come to a consensus that, broadly speaking, all societies can be grouped into two major camps in terms of governance environment: the ones that have good *public ordering*, or rule of law, and the ones that do not have good public ordering.[5] While readers from the West are familiar with the first type, they are unfamiliar with the latter, for some obvious reasons, which we will discuss in more detail in this book.

What do people rely on to protect their property rights and other interests in economic exchanges if the public laws are no good? Well, it really depends. If the public ordering (i.e., public laws and government enforcement) is ineffective, the society must rely on some sort of private ordering in order to make certain (minimally) necessary economic activities feasible. But private ordering can have many forms. Some may be conducive to business, and others may be hostile or even dangerous to conducting business. For instance, ordering can be based on a dictatorship imposed by a military strongman who monopolizes all business opportunities. Ordering can also be in a state of complete anarchy, in which bandits roam and rob people and make business activities based on free and voluntary exchange virtually impossible.

Ordering can also be based on an extensive informal social network among businesses maintained by tradition or private enforcement, which may function effectively and efficiently under certain conditions. It is this type of particular private ordering that has drawn increasing attention from social scientists. Among the efforts at studying private ordering, a new and useful approach is to compare the two major types of governance system to reveal not-so-obvious yet important patterns that may help us understand systematically how different countries conduct economic exchanges in their particular ways of interacting. This approach is called "rule-based versus relation-based governance."

A New Perspective: Rule-Based and Relation-Based Governance Systems

The framework of rule-based and relation-based governance systems was first proposed by Shuhe Li and later was expanded on by others.[6] According to the framework, if we examine the governance environment at the societal level from political, legal, economic, and social perspectives, we can derive two contrasting systems, *rule-based* versus *relation-based*, in terms of how people protect their property rights and contracts.

In most developed societies, we observe that firms and individuals primarily rely on public rules—laws and government regulations—to resolve disputes and enforce rights and contracts. We call this reliance on public ordering a *rule-based governance system*. A rule-based governance environment must satisfy the following conditions: the public rules governing economic exchanges (such as laws, state policies, and regulations) are fairly made; the rule-making, rule-adjudication, and rule-enforcement are separate; rule-enforcement is fair and efficient; and public information infrastructure (such as accounting, auditing, and financial rating) is highly reliable and accurate. That the public information must be of high quality and trustworthy is vital for a rule-based economy to function smoothly and efficiently. Firms and people must be able to rely on publicly available information such as financial analyses and auditing reports in order to conduct business and make decisions, saving the cost of privately collecting information and investigating its quality for every potential business transaction. An important feature of relying on public information is that the information must be *explicit* and verifiable by a third party; otherwise, it cannot be admitted in court if disputes arise. The court can only enforce the agreements between the parties that are publicly (third-party) verifiable; any implicit agreements privately made between them that cannot be verified by the court are not admissible to the court and thus cannot be enforced. As a result, business agreements in a rule-based society are usually formal and clearly written in explicit language. Because of the above conditions, citizens and organizations predominantly rely on public ordering in governing transactions.

The above features imply that rule-based societies tend to be mature democracies. For instance, for the laws and rules to be fair, a society must ensure fair participation of all interest groups in law making, which requires a representative democracy. For legal interpretation to be impartial, judges must be independent of political influence, which implies checks and balances between different branches of the government, and for the enforcement to be impartial and efficient, the executive branch has to be answerable to the constituents and be checked by the legislative and judiciary branches. This is why mature democracies share many commonalities, while nondemocracies may take many forms, ranging from monarchy, to military rule, to communist rule, to civil war and anarchy. Rule-based societies tend to have similar rules, yet non-rule-based societies may take different forms of private enforcement mechanisms to govern transactions (e.g., community enforcement, private network enforcement, kinship enforcement, or mafia-dominated enforcement). In other words, while rule-based societies converge to the profile described above (e.g., highly rule-based societies are all mature democracies), societies that lack a rule-based governance environment vary widely, ranging from warring states with complete chaos to tightly controlled societies under highly efficient authoritarian rules.

We observe that a specific group of non-rule-based societies that rely on private ordering (e.g., the East Asian societies in general and the Chinese society in particular) are quite effective and efficient at governing the social exchanges that have been experiencing rapid economic growth. In addition to the absence of fair and efficient public rules due to the lack of any of the above-mentioned conditions necessary to a rule-based governance system, these societies have the following in common: They all have a governance environment based on private enforcement that can effectively and efficiently regulate markets and resolve disputes. This is what we call a *relation-based governance system*.

A relation-based society has the following characteristics: public rules (laws, government policies, and government regulations) are less fair because they are usually biased in favor of certain privileged groups (due to the lack of checks and balances); the executive branch of the government usually overshadows the legislative and judiciary branches and is likely to be controlled by a dictatorial ruling elite; courts and judges are controlled by the ruler(s); government operations are secretive and public information and press are controlled and censored by the government; industries and markets tend to be controlled by a small number of insiders (e.g., people who have connections with the ruler) and are closed to outsiders; officials and business insiders are usually locked in a corruption-bribery relationship; and the informal network among the insiders in an industry is so closely knit and powerful that if one of the insiders is said to have broken the (unwritten) norms of the trade, the word of mouth by other insiders will effectively put him out of business.

For example, in Thailand, a relation-based society, there exists a class of powerful businessmen called "*chao pho*," or godfathers.[7] They "cultivate close links with local officialdom . . . to secure the licenses, permits, land deeds . . . to corner the lucrative government contracts."[8] These godfathers also provide "some measure of security [and] justice . . . more speedily and more accessibly than officialdom." Also, "whenever these [ordinary] people have any problems they go to the *chao pho*."[9] Similar private social networks have also existed in Malaysia. Historically, because the government was unable to provide many public services, residents, especially the Chinese there, began to form a *sherh-hui-tarng*, commonly known as a "secret society," to help each other in political, economic, and legal matters.[10] Vietnam, as a seasoned business writer summed up, relied on an "informal system of rule by people, rather than rule by law."[11]

How Do People Govern Transactions in a Relation-Based Society?

Unlike a rule-based society, where public information is credible and heavily relied upon by citizens and businesses (making the protection of business transactions by public ordering feasible and efficient), public information in a relation-based society is usually untrustworthy. As a result, people and firms rely on private information to govern their transactions. There are several reasons why public information is not trusted. First, the government controls public information and the media in order to support its rule and agenda. For instance, it is well known that the governments in China and Vietnam (both are relation-based societies) tightly control the media and decide what news can be published.[12] They even doctor news stories and time news releases in order to reinforce their rules. For instance, news of major scientific discoveries is often saved and released on major political holidays (e.g., the National Day, the Communist Party's birthday). The practice of manipulating public information at the national level by the government does not help firms to report accurate information. As we will show later in the book, there is strong evidence that firms in relation-based societies such as China manipulate their income reports.[13]

Another reason why public information is rarely useful as a means for firms to govern their transactions is the nature of these transactions. When the scale of the economy is small and business people predominately deal with people they know, they rely on private information between the transacting parties and they do not want to make their information available to a third party because the private business relationship is their most important asset. It is a small wonder that when researchers in Thailand interviewed successful business people about their political activities, few were willing to talk about it.[14] Similar patterns were also found among successful Chinese business people.[15]

Such private relationships and information usually are *local* and *implicit*, and the agreement (e.g., a handshake or a pat on the shoulder) is most often *informal* and cannot be verified by a third party such as a judge in a court. These practices, as we discussed earlier, are the opposite of rule-based governance, and as a result, business people must rely on private means to protect their transaction. Specifically, firms in a relation-based society rely on three private monitoring mechanisms to govern their rights in transactions: These mechanisms are *ex ante* monitoring capability, *interim* (also called *ex nunc*) monitoring capability, and *ex post* monitoring capability.

Ex ante means "before the event" and is used in economic analysis to forecast the results of a particular action. Private *ex ante* monitoring capability refers to the effort invested by a transaction party *before* a business deal is made. In the absence of public information and enforcement, a firm must privately investigate its prospective transaction partner in terms of his or her track record and reputation. If the prospect has cheated, do not deal with him. If the prospective partner does not have a stable pool of business partners or clients, it implies that he may have a bad reputation and is avoided by other insiders. Such a prospect should be ruled out.

Interim monitoring is the ability of one party to obtain ongoing business and operational information about the other party, specifically whether the other party is on track with a project's schedule or whether the other party has any financial trouble or disputes. In a relation-based society, such information is not publicly available through credit investigating agencies. This is why news of financial insolvency of a firm in a relation-based society tends to cause large-scale panic. Due to the lack of reliable public financial data, people do not know whether other firms may also be involved with the insolvent firm and are thus adversely affected. As a result, people stop lending to or withdrawing deposits from firms likely to be involved with the insolvent firm (a snowball effect). Therefore, one must invest in the capability of obtaining private and reliable information.

The third monitoring mechanism, private *ex post* capability, is the most important of the three. *Ex post*, Latin for "after the fact," is used here to refer to the ability to remedy or deter cheating or other opportunistic behaviors by the other party, in the absence of resorting to public regulators such as the courts (which tend to be corrupt, unfair, and inefficient in relation-based societies). In a relation-based society it is not uncommon for a promisee to resort to kidnapping in order to force a promisor to fulfill a promissory obligation (which may be an implicit, oral promise). For relation-based governance to work efficiently, private *ex post* monitoring must be effective and efficient. A *New York Times* report about informal, relation-based lending in China vividly describes such *ex post* monitoring:

> Borrowers default on nearly half the loans issued by the state-owned banks, but seldom do so here on money that is usually borrowed from relatives, neighbors or people in the same industry. Residents insist that the risk of ostracism for failing to repay a loan is penalty enough to ensure repayment of most loans . . . [As one lender puts it], "If it weren't a good friend, I wouldn't lend the money . . ." Violence is extremely rare, but the threat of it does exist as the ultimate guarantor that people make every effort to repay debts. "Someone can hire a killer who will chase you down, beat you up and maybe even kill you."[16]

In Thailand, the powerful business people—godfathers—"built up networks of associates and gangs of subordinates." Because they took the law in their own hands, the areas in which they dominated "acquired a reputation for hired gunmen, sporadic violence, and regular newspaper reports of murders 'arising out of a business dispute.'"[17]

In Vietnam, experienced business people all know that a formal contract is not very useful. "If the contract is not conducted satisfactorily," a successful Vietnamese entrepreneur commented, "we have the option to sue them, but that would be ridiculous. You know the legal system here."[18]

The Costs and Benefits of a Relation-Based Governance System

Since we observe that all advanced countries rely on public rules for governance, we may be tempted to rush to the conclusion that relation-based governance is categorically inefficient and thus detrimental to economic development. However, such a conclusion is premature. Relation-based governance systems are not all inefficient and thus hinder economic growth. Under certain conditions, relation-based governance can be quite effective and efficient due to its differing cost structure.

A well-functioning rule-based system is not free of cost to build and use. Imagine, for instance, the public ordering in the United States, one of the most advanced rule-based countries, and the infrastructure it must have in order for public ordering to function effectively and efficiently. In general, public ordering needs the establishment of the three-branch government. First of all, the country must build a legislative body, which in the United States means establishing and organizing the House and the Senate in Congress, the election system in all 50 states to select all the senators and representatives, and the infrastructure that supports the operations of legislation in Congress. Second, the country must build a court system ranging from the Supreme Court to local courts that are autonomous and well funded. This infrastructure compels the society to invest in an education system that can train a sufficiently large number of judges who are professional, ethical, impartial, and well paid. The society must also invest in training an army of lawyers and other legal workers with high professional and ethical standards. Last but not least, public ordering requires a credible and powerful law enforcement branch—the executive branch of the government, including a police force that must be well trained, adequately paid, and thus uncorrupted.

Simply put, *a well-functioning rule-based system requires a large investment in legal infrastructure* that is costly and takes a long time to build. From a cost accounting perspective, such an investment at the national level can be viewed as a *fixed cost* That does not vary regardless of how many people use it. Once the legal infrastructure is built and functioning, *the incremental cost of drafting and enforcing one more contract is relatively low*. In other words, whether the legal system enforces one contract or 1 million contracts, the fixed, upfront investment for the legal infrastructure is the same (and *sunk* in the sense that it cannot be recovered), and the *marginal cost* (the incremental cost of enforcing an additional contract) is minimal.

Meanwhile, *in a relation-based society, business can thrive with minimal social order*. As long as crimes such as robberies are not out of control, business can be conducted and governed by well-functioning social-industrial networks maintained by private players (individuals or firms). In Thailand, where the public protection of business is not very effective or efficient and the formal channel of financing (through banks) is expensive because of stringent rules, the Chinese Thai business community has resorted to informal financing among themselves. As one researcher observed, "Chinese [Thai] merchants . . . could inform themselves much more efficiently than branch offices of Bangkok banks about the credit status of other local Chinese . . . Their businesses were based on personal relationships . . . They arranged [private financing] to cut down fellow businessmen's transaction costs . . . Ultimately, they helped to increase the efficiency of Chinese business transactions and to redress a resource allocation distorted by economic regulation."[19]

Another interesting difference in contract fulfillment and enforcement between the two systems is that, unlike public enforcement of contracts, which relies on third-party verifiable information that may be only part (the written part) of the general agreement between two parties, private enforcement is based on private information, which may not need to be verified by a third party. In this sense, private enforcement can be more complete than public enforcement, even including implicit agreements based on mutual understanding, the spirit of cooperation, or past practices.

In general, compared to the cost structure of the rule-based system, the relation-based governance system incurs few fixed costs (since it does not rely on a nationwide legal infrastructure). But *the marginal (incremental) cost of privately enforcing contracts increases as the scale and scope of one's business expands.* For example, if one only does business with his siblings, the marginal cost of the three types of monitoring (*ex ante*, interim, and *ex post*) is low, because he knows their reputation, their ability to deliver, and where their assets are (in case he needs to seize them). But when his business grows and he runs out of family members, he may have to deal with people he does not know as well, such as neighbors or distant relatives, and his marginal cost of monitoring increases. In general, the marginal (incremental) cost of establishing new relationships rises because cultivating new relationships becomes more and more expensive and time-consuming when one's private network expands from family members to strangers. For this reason, in a relation-based society people first do business with family members and then with friends and people they know. They try to avoid dealing with strangers because it takes a long time to develop close relationships, and the costs of private monitoring and enforcement are high.

Therefore, *when the scale and scope of the economy are small, relation-based governance may be effective and efficient,* as the society avoids costly investment in developing and maintaining the legal infrastructures. People and firms are constrained to and content with dealing with family members, friends, and people in closely knit circles. As illustrated in

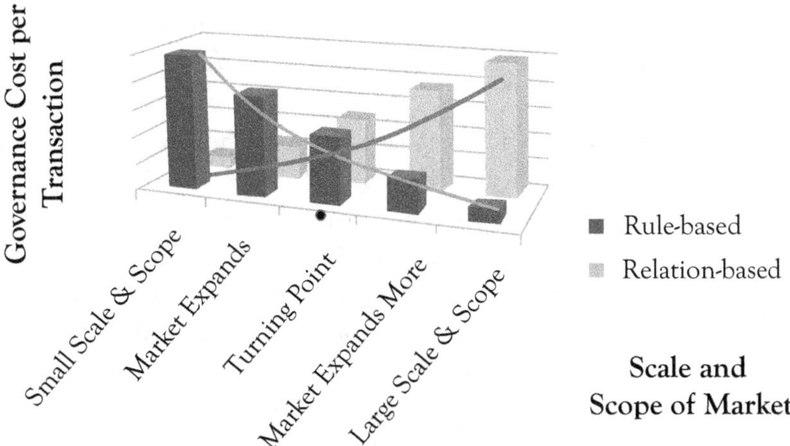

Figure 1.1. The governance cost of rule-based and relation-based systems

Figure 1.1, when the market is small, the average governance cost is lower in relation-based societies, giving them a comparative advantage during the take-off stage of their economy.

However, when an economy expands from local to national and international scope, the relation-based governance becomes inefficient. The average cost of finding and establishing new relationships rises, and thus the average cost of governance surpasses that of rule-based economies, as illustrated at the turning point in Figure 1.1. At this point, a relation-based society begins to lose its comparative advantage in governance costs to a rule-based society. It faces the pressure to evolve into a rule-based governance environment. A postponement of the transition caused by resistance from people who are deeply entrenched and vested in the existing relational network hinders a country's economic development. This point will be further elaborated later.

We now have a clearer idea regarding the question on the "East Asian economic miracle": These countries have extensive informal social networks that enable them to rely on the relation-based system to govern economic activities. This system has helped them to save the huge fixed costs of building an effective public governance system. In other words, they did not have to wait until they could build a vast, expensive legal infrastructure for their economy to take off. These countries have relied on private governance mechanisms maintained and enforced by family members, friends, cronies, and related people in high places (possibly through bribery) to protect their business interests and operations. *The "East Asian economic miracle" has been achieved with the help of the relation-based governance system.*

Furthermore, we can now see that the Chinese heavily rely on *guanxi* (Chinese for connection and relation) in business activities not only because of their cultural heritage but also and more importantly, because the public rules are not effective and efficient in providing fair protection for their property rights and interests. *Relying on the relation-based way to conduct business activities is not merely a cultural phenomenon, it is fundamentally determined by the stage of political and economic development in a society.* Relying on private relations to settle business disputes is not unique to East Asian societies. Historically, feudal Europe and the United States were primarily relation-based societies.[20] Contemporarily,

Table 1.1. Differences Between Relation-Based and Rule-Based Governance

Relation-based governance	Rule-based governance
Relying on private and local information	Relying on public information
Complete enforcement possible	Enforcing a subset of observable agreements
Implicit and nonverifiable agreements	Explicit and third-party verifiable agreements
Requiring minimum social order	Requiring well-developed legal infrastructure
Low fixed costs to set up the system	High fixed costs to set up the system
High and increasing marginal costs to maintain	Low and decreasing marginal costs to maintain
Effective in small and emerging economies	Effective in large and advanced economies

Source: Based on Li (2004a).

Table 1.2. Types of Governance and Economic Systems

Degree to which a society relies on relation-based governance	Degree to which a society relies on rule-based governance	
	Low	High
Low	(Type D) Countries that have weak informal social networks or live in chaos or civil wars (e.g., some Latin American and African countries)	(Type A) Most mature market economies (United States, Western Europe)
High	(Type B) Certain developing and transition economies that have strong extended informal social networks (e.g., China, Vietnam, Thailand)	(Type C) Economies that mix rule-based system with strong relation-based culture (e.g., Hong Kong, Singapore*)

* It can be argued that both Hong Kong and Singapore were relation-based and have evolved into a more rule-based environment. However, due to their link with China and their Chinese cultural heritage, they are familiar with and may still use the relation-based way to conduct business.

Source: Based on Li, Park, and Li (2004).

many developing and transition economies such as Mexico, Mali, and Zambia are relation-based even though they do not have the Chinese or East Asian cultural heritage (see chapter 2).

Table 1.1 highlights the main contrasting features of the two systems we have discussed so far. We will discuss them in more detail in the book.

In Table 1.2, we examine the interface of the two systems. Based on the rule-based versus relation-based framework, we can make a typology of four types of societies: (a) societies that rely on rule-based governance system (most developed countries); (b) societies that lack fair and efficient public rules and rely on relation-based governance environment (developing countries with strong relation-based networks); (c) societies that are rule-based and yet have strong relation-based networks (such as Hong Kong); and (d) societies that lack fair and efficient public rules and do not have efficient and effective relation-based networks either (e.g., countries in civil war or chaos).

Caution: Rule-Based Versus Relation-Based Societies Are Not Black and White

It should be noted that all human societies, including relation-based ones, have various degrees of formal rules. When we say a country is relation-based, it does not mean that this country has no formal laws. Even the most lawless country must have a set of published legal codes of some sort. But the state may not follow the laws and the ruler may simply ignore them. What distinguishes relation-based societies from rule-based ones is not who has the most comprehensive written laws, it is that people in relation-based societies tend to *circumvent* formal rules because the rules and the enforcement tend to be unfair, particularistic (depending on who has better relationship with people in power), and corrupt.

Another caveat is the distinction between the relation-based governance system and the relational business practice. By our definition, relying on a relation-based governance system is to use private means to fulfill the social function of protecting property rights, such as enforcing contracts, usually done by the government in societies where public ordering functions well. Thus, strictly speaking, relying on relation-based governance is to ignore the public law at best or violate it at worst, even though the law itself may be unfair or inefficient. In other words, resorting to the relation-based governance system implies that one must break existing laws in some way.

Relational business means conducting business though private relationships, such as knowing one's customers in person and matching individual customer's need with a service uniquely tailored for the customer. It does not necessarily mean to circumvent the law. Thus the relation-based governance system, which is the main focus of this book, is different from relational business (such as relational marketing).

Throughout the book, we will show that the relation-based governance system is distinctive and yet intertwined with its counterpart, the rule-based system, and the relationship between the two is complicated. As the book unfolds, the reader will be able to see that the logic we use to explain the relationship is rather simple and powerful. Some economic phenomena that apparently contradict economic theories, such as why foreign investment pours into countries with a poor legal system, can be more logically and convincingly explained.

CHAPTER 2

Distinguishing Rule-Based and Relation-Based Countries

How to Measure Governance Environment

Chapter 1 gives us an overview of the theory of rule-based and relation-based governance. An immediate question is, which countries are rule-based and which are relation-based? For instance, if we consider entering the market of India, how do we know whether it is rule-based or relation-based? In this chapter, we will discuss how to evaluate whether a country is relatively more rule-based or relation-based, and we will measure the governance environments of the countries on which we have data. For business readers, understanding the criteria that we use to evaluate the governance system will provide a tool to assess the business environment of a target country in the future.

Measuring Rule-Based Governance: The Governance Environment Index (GEI)

Based on the literature on governance environment, we created a Governance Environment Index (GEI), which is a sum of five governance-related indicators:[1] political rights, rule of law, free flow of information, quality of accounting standards, and public trust, which are explained in more detail below.

1. *Political rights*. This indicator measures the political rights available to a country's citizens. The more political rights citizens have (as opposed to the political power of the rulers), the more democratic

the political system is, which provides more checks and balances among the political forces. Thus sufficient political rights are the foundation for the rule-based governance system.

2. *Rule of law.* This indicator measures the degree to which a country has the rule of law. As we discussed earlier, a fair, effective, and efficient legal system is a necessary condition for citizens to rely on public ordering, or rule-based governance, to solve disputes and protect property rights.

3. *Free flow of information* (as opposed to government control over the flow of information) is a necessary condition for a rule-based society, as it depends on high-quality, publicly available economic information. It is assumed that if information can be freely disseminated in a country, the competition among all sources of information will force the information providers to offer more accurate and timely information. On the other hand, if the state controls and censors information, then the quality of publicly available information will be poor and people will trust it less.

4. *Quality of accounting standards.* This indicator, closely related to the free flow of information, specifically measures the quality of publicly verifiable financial information such as company financial disclosure and auditing, which are fundamental for a rule-based governance to work efficiently.

5. *Public trust (generalized trust).* To put it simply, trust is a confidence one places in the other person's reliability. Public trust, or generalized trust, is the belief that most people, including strangers, can be trusted. A higher level of public trust reduces the cost of information verification and the cost of sanctioning cheaters, making rule-based enforcement efficient. Based on the same rationale, political scientists find that a high level of public trust is conducive to democracy, which, in its mature form, is a highly rule-based governance system.

All the five indicators are positively correlated with a rule-based governance environment. In other words, the higher the degrees of political rights, rule of law, free flow of information, quality of accounting standards, and public trust, the higher the degree of rule-based governance in a country. (Please see the appendix for detailed information on the data sources of the five indicators.) Based on the five indicators, we create the GEI, which is the sum of the standardized value of the five indicators.

Table 2.1 lists the GEI of all the countries for which we have available data.

The GEI measures the degree to which a country is rule-based. It is a relative measure. For example, based on Table 2.1, we can say that compared to Egypt, the United Kingdom is more rule-based. The countries that are ranked at the top, such as Finland, Sweden, and the Netherlands, are the most rule-based countries, whereas the countries at the bottom, namely Iran, China, and Vietnam, are the least rule-based. Since the GEI score is constructed by the sum of the five standardized indicators,

Table 2.1. GEI by Country

Country	GEI	Country	GEI
Finland	6.41	Taiwan	−0.13
Sweden	6.18	Romania	−0.63
Netherlands	5.70	Thailand	−0.84
Germany	4.53	India	−0.85
United Kingdom	4.35	Ukraine	−0.86
Switzerland	4.34	Indonesia	−1.10
New Zealand	4.04	Bulgaria	−1.75
Hong Kong	4.02	Mali	−1.81
Australia	3.73	Peru	−1.92
South Africa	3.11	Brazil	−2.06
United States	2.30	Zambia	−2.64
Cyprus	2.28	Turkey	−2.75
Slovenia	2.23	Argentina	−2.75
France	1.97	Malaysia	−2.91
Japan	1.79	Egypt	−3.04
Poland	1.32	Moldova	−3.43
Spain	1.18	Colombia	−3.69
Ghana	0.95	Morocco	−3.70
Italy	0.94	Mexico	−3.71
South Korea	0.24	Russia	−4.34
Trinidad & Tobago	0.12	Vietnam	−5.19
Chile	0.12	China	−5.92
		Iran	−8.13

the mean of GEI is zero. The simplest way to categorize the countries in Table 2.1 is to divide them into two groups, one with positive GEIs and the other with negative GEIs. We may say that the countries with a positive GEI are more rule-based and the ones with a negative GEI are less rule-based.[2] Countries with high GEIs, or rule-based countries, are characterized by strong political rights, the rule of law, free flow of information, high public trust, and high quality of accounting standards.

An important caveat is that the GEI only measures how much a country is rule-based; it does not measure to what extent a country is relation-based. A negative GEI means that the country is less rule-based, but it does not mean that it must be relation-based. Some less rule-based countries are relation-based and some are not. We need to find a way to distinguish them.

Measuring Relation-Based Governance

As we discussed earlier, a country that is not rule-based may not necessarily be relation-based; it can be governed by anything but public rules. Conceivably, there are countries that have neither strong public rules nor extensive informal social networks (i.e., relation-based governance) to conduct and protect business. More generally, how do we distinguish which countries are more relation-based among the non-rule-based countries?

Based on the literature, a key indicator that can help us to do this is the level of trust in a country. Broadly speaking, there are two types of trust in terms of *who* people trust: *generalized trust* (also called public trust, as we have reviewed earlier) and *particularized trust*.[3] People who have generalized trust believe that most people, including strangers, can be trusted. If a society has a high level of generalized trust, then the cost of testing and verifying the integrity of prospective business partners will be lower, thus increasing economic efficiency for a society. Data show that affluent societies—countries with high economic development level—have high levels of generalized trust, as shown in Figure 2.1. From the perspective of the political system, a higher level of generalized trust means that people have confidence that others will abide by the rule of law and cooperate in maintaining it. This confidence will make a pluralistic political system such as democracy work more efficiently.

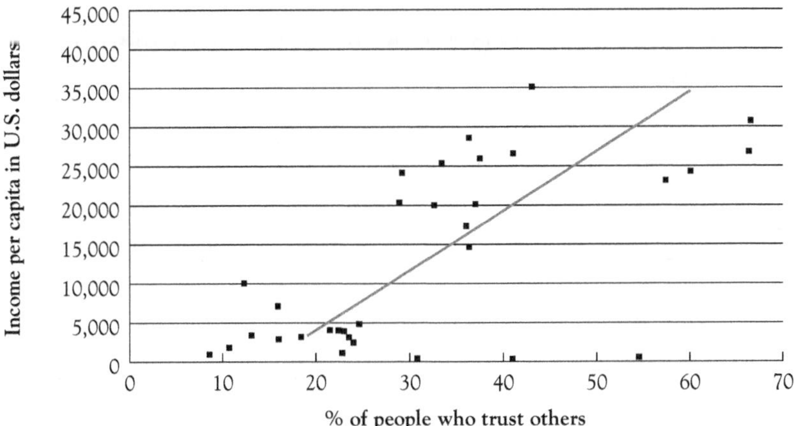

Figure 2.1. Trust and income level

Note: X = % of people who trust others. Y = Income per capita in U.S. dollars. Each observation is a country.

Sources: World Bank (2000); World Value Survey (2005).

On the contrary, in countries with low economic development and weak rule of law, the level of generalized trust tends to be low (Figure 2.2) and there seems to be mutually reinforcing interaction between the two: the lack of generalized trust creates more friction in the political and economic activities in a country, which, in turn, makes economic activities less efficient.

When a society does not have sufficiently high levels of generalized trust, it must have another kind of trust to make social exchanges possible. As economics Nobel Prize laureate Kenneth Arrow stated succinctly, "Virtually every commercial transaction has within itself an element of trust."[4] When people have very little confidence or faith in strangers, they rely on people they know well, such as family members or close friends. Such trust is called *particularized trust.* People who adhere to particularized trust do not believe that people in general can be trusted. They only trust the people they know through certain groups (networks) to which they belong, such as relatives, friends, or members of one's club. In general, particularized trust is based on the close relationship one has with the person to be trusted (so that they easily be held accountable). Implicitly, maintaining particularized trust relies on the three monitoring

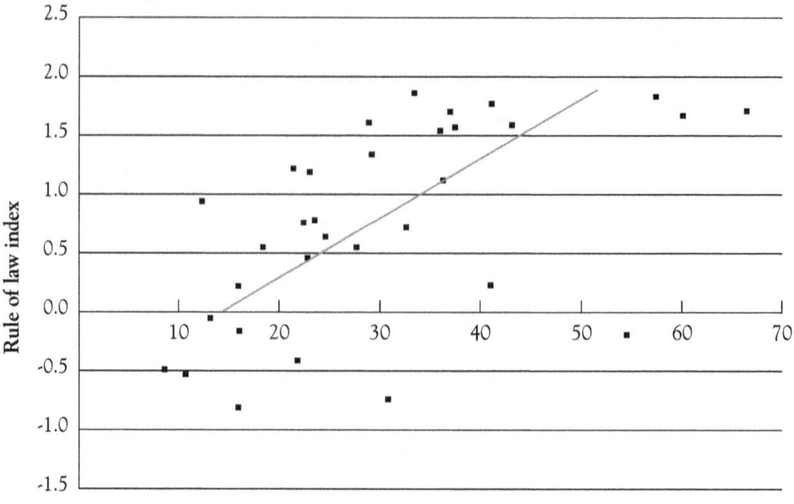

Figure 2.2. Trust and rule of law

Note: X = % of people who trust others. Y = Rule of Law Index (high value = high degree of rule of law). Each observation is a country.

Sources: Gwartney and Lawson.(2002); World Value Survey (2005).

mechanisms discussed in the introduction: *ex ante*, interim, and *ex post*. For example, X can trust Y only because X knows Y's history well (Y should not have a bad record in business dealings), can follow up with Y's ongoing activities, and can punish him if he cheats.

Upon further examination, we find that the closeness, or the distance, of one's relationship varies. The closest relationship is among the direct members of the family: spouse, parents, and children. The second closest relationship may be with relatives such as in-laws, cousins, and other close family. Friends, neighbors, and coworkers usually belong to the next circle. The level of particularized trust people place on these different relationships varies across societies.

Take the case of the Chinese society, for example. The conventional view is that the Chinese put paramount importance on the family and rely almost exclusively on family ties to conduct and safeguard their business. This view is actually quite misleading. Recent studies and surveys on the sources of particularized trust in China have revealed that the Chinese place more trust in neighbors and friends than in family.[5]

Such relationship building was practiced among Chinese Thais in Thailand. As observed by researchers of the Chinese Thais, "They invested in one another's enterprises to share risks and rewards, and they exchanged marriage partners to strengthen links, often with little reference to traditional boundaries on such alliances."[6]

The Chinese *guanxi* culture is not about trusting family members only; it is about relying on an extended informal social network of friends and friends' friends to conduct business and protect property rights. In China, for historical reasons, the *guanxi* culture is very strong. Everyone must have his or her circle of close friends. The members of the circle help each other in social interactions and exchanges. The mutual help is effectively and efficiently enforced through the three monitoring mechanisms (*ex ante*, interim, and *ex post*) with minimal costs, since the members know each other well. This familiarity includes knowledge of one's history in dealings (so to exclude cheaters) and asset information (in case it is necessary to seize someone's assets as compensation). In China, almost everyone must belong to a circle in order to survive. (People who do not belong to any close circles tend to be the ones with questionable history or shady character, such as having cheated, and thus are avoided by others.) Therefore, the Chinese society can be viewed as consisting of numerous circles of close friends. Resourceful people are the ones who belong to multiple circles. They act as liaisons to link different circles by introducing members of one circle to another. And this kind of introduction is very powerful; it is not merely a friend introducing someone to a new friend, it is to link two or more circles together, with minimal monitoring cost for potential cheating. For example, X is a member of both Circles A and B. His friend Y in Circle A needs access to someone in Circle B for, say, applying for a special license. X then introduces Y to Z, who is in Circle B and therefore a friend of X. Once the introduction is done, then Y and Z can have almost instant trust in each other, because the monitoring cost between them is low. If Z cheats Y, then Y can punish X easily in Circle A, and X can in turn punish Z in Circle B. If Z were kicked out of Circle B, it would be devastating in a society in which people's livelihood heavily relies on such circles. This strong deterrence will ensure that Z will not cheat.

The case of secret societies in Malaysia provides further evidence on such cross memberships. It is not uncommon for the members of a family to join different societies so that the family gets "the best of both worlds" in a sense that it can get protection and business opportunities from all the societies the members have joined.[7]

When a researcher in Vietnam interviewed a "highly successful land broker," he attributed his success to an informal network resulting from "shared history through alma maters, military services, neighborhood associations, parties, anniversaries, and memorial services that bring people together."[8] Interestingly, he did not mention the word "family." In another study on trust and interfirm relationships in Vietnam, the authors found that an important way to quickly establish trust and a close relationship between two new partners is through a third party. A natural way to start a conversation between two prospective partners is to find a mutual friend and talk about their relationship with the mutual acquaintance. As a Vietnamese business executive commented, "It is easier to talk about common friends. But more importantly, we feel more secure when there are [*sic*] someone who knows both of us."[9]

Particularized trust that goes beyond family members and extends to neighbors, friends, and friends' friends can be termed *extended* particularized trust. These thick private networks based on the extended particularized trust that overlap among them and reach every corner of a society make up what we call *relation-based governance*.

Societies That Lack Extended Particularized Trust

There are also societies that lack trust of any kind. People there don't have much confidence or faith in anyone. But in order to conduct business, they have to rely on someone. In such a situation, family members come in handy, and the saying "blood is thicker than water" makes the most sense. In general, when the society has extremely low levels of trust, people predominately rely on family members to conduct business and protect property rights. Borrowing from the sociological term "nuclear family," we refer to the narrow particularized trust that is only applied to family members as *nuclear* particularized trust. Correspondingly, the type of governance environment that is associated with nuclear particularized trust is not relation-based; we will call it "family-based."

Family-based governance is more primitive than relation-based governance because the economic cooperation is limited to family members only and may not always be the most efficient choice. For example, within a family business, the key posts are held by family members who may not be best qualified, and in firm-to-firm or government-to-firm relationships, a government official or a firm's head tends to award projects to a firm owned by his family, which may not be the most efficient or highest quality (this will be further discussed in chapter 7).

Therefore, we can distinguish relation-based countries from non-relation-based countries by examining the dominant type of particularized trust. The countries that have a relatively high level of extended particularized trust are relation-based. In other words, people in relation-based countries tend to have a high level of trust beyond trusting family members only; they also place a high level of trust on nonfamily friends such as neighbors. Table 2.2 summarizes our categorization of trusts.

Based on the above rationale, we conducted a clustering analysis of the 23 countries that have negative GEIs (the non-rule-based countries) based on the types of particularized trust in each country. The main criteria we used for the clustering analysis include indicators of generalized trust, indicators of trust on family, friends, and people one meets for the first time. Table 2.3 shows the result of the clustering analysis.

On average, as compared to those in Cluster 2, Cluster 1 countries have (a) a higher level of generalized trust, (b) a slightly lower level of trust in family, and (c) a higher level of trust in neighbors and people one meets for the first time. They fit our description of relation-based

Table 2.2. Types of Trust

Type of trust		Domain of trust	Corresponding governance environment
Generalized trust		Most people, including strangers, foreigners, people of different religion	Rule-based; to a lesser extent relation-based
Particularized trust	Extended particularized trust	Neighbors, people who are introduced by someone you know	Relation-based
	Nuclear particularized trust	Only one's family	Less relation-based; more family-based

Table 2.3. Clustering of More Relation-Based Versus More Family-Based Countries

Country	Cluster	Country	Cluster
China	1	Argentina	2
Indonesia	1	Brazil	2
Malaysia	1	Bulgaria	2
Mali	1	Colombia	2
Mexico	1	Egypt	2
Taiwan	1	India	2
Thailand	1	Iran	2
Vietnam	1	Moldova	2
Zambia	1	Morocco	2
		Peru	2
		Romania	2
		Russia	2
		Turkey	2
		Ukraine	2

Note: 1 = more relation-based; 2 = more family-based.

countries. In comparison, Cluster 2 countries have slightly higher trust in family and lower trust in other trust measures. These are countries in which most people do not rely on public rules or extended private relations.

Because the clustering results may differ based on the method used, the clustering variables, and the number of clusters, we experimented with different methods, different sets of clustering variables, and different numbers of clusters. While the memberships vary, some members are always clustered together. Countries that always ended up in Cluster 1 (the relation-based type) are China, Taiwan, Vietnam, and Indonesia. Morocco, Iran, and India tend to cluster at the other end. This pattern is also confirmed by simple ranking based on one of the most specific trust questions in the 2005 World Value Survey, Question V47: "Do you think most people would try to take advantage of you if they got a chance, or would they try to be fair?" Relation-based countries have a higher percentage of respondents who believe that people try to be fair (see the rankings in Table 2.4).

Table 2.4. Ranking of Relation-Based Countries

Country	Trust score	Country	Trust score
Vietnam	6.16	Ukraine	3.60
China	5.92	Egypt	3.36
Indonesia	5.09	Colombia	3.26
Taiwan	5.08	Argentina	3.12
Thailand	4.53	Brazil	3.10
Mexico	4.46	Romania	3.07
Mali	4.33	Bulgaria	2.82
Malaysia	4.12	Iran	2.80
Zambia	4.01	Turkey	2.75
Moldova	3.88	India	2.35
Russia	3.65	Morocco	2.02
Peru	3.63		

Note: Scores are average answers by each country. A high score means people in a country incline to agree that "people try to be fair," indicating the country is more relation-based; a low score means people in a country incline to agree that "people try to take advantage of me," indicating it is less relation-based.

In this book, we will focus on the more relation-based countries, such as China, Taiwan, Indonesia, Thailand, and Malaysia and contrast them with rule-based countries when we discuss how business is conducted, managed, and protected.

Appendix 1. Data Sources of Calculating the GEI

Indicator	Description	Source
Political rights	Adopted from the Freedom House survey of "Freedom in the World." The survey asks 10 political rights questions in three categories: (a) electoral process, (b) political pluralism and participation, and (c) functioning of government. The raw points are then used to calculate the score of political rights in a country. It ranges from 1 (highest amount of political rights for citizens) to 7 (lowest).	Freedom House, http://www.freedomhouse.org/template.cfm?page=15
Rule of law	Derived from the *Economic Freedom of the World Annual Report* by J. Gwartney and R. Lawson. It measures the degree to which the court system in a country is impartial. It ranges from 1 (least impartial) to 10 (most impartial).	Economic Freedom of the World Annual Report by J. Gwartney and R. Lawson, http://www.cato.org/pubs/efw/
Free flow of information	Based on the "Press Freedom Index," which measures the degree of freedom journalists and media have in more than 160 countries. It is based on annual surveys that ask 50 questions in 7 areas: (a) physical attacks, imprisonment, and direct threats on journalists and media assistants; (b) indirect threats and access to information; (c) legal situation and unjustified prosecution; (d) censorship, self-censorship; (e) public media; (f) economic and administrative pressure; (g) the Internet and new media. The score ranges from 0 (most free) to over 100 (least free).	Reporters Without Borders, http://www.rsf.org/en -classement554–2005.html
Quality of accounting standards	Based on the 2008 Deloitte report on the adoption of the International Financial Report Standard (IFRS) across countries. The indicator ranges from 1 (not adopting IFRS—low standard) to 4 (compete adoption—high standard), with 2 and 3 indicating partial adoption.	Deloitte, "Use of IFRS for reporting by domestic listed companies by country and region," http://www.iasplus.com/country/useias.htm
Public trust	Adopted from the 2005 World Value Survey conducted by Inglehart al et. The indicator is derived from the replies to the question following Question V23: "Generally speaking, would you say that most people can be trusted or that you need to be very careful in dealing with people?" 1 = "most people can be trusted," and 2 = "need to be very careful."	World Value Survey, http://www .worldvaluessurvey.org/

Appendix 2. Data Used to Measure the Types of Trust

Type of trust		Measurement (variable) used	Source
Generalized trust		V23: "Generally speaking, would you say that most people can be trusted or that you need to be very careful in dealing with people?" 1 = "most people can be trusted," and 2 = "need to be very careful." V47: "Do you think most people would try to take advantage of you if they got a chance, or would they try to be fair?" 1 = "try to take advantage of you," and 7 = "try to be fair."	2005 World Value Survey
Particularized trust	Extended particularized trust	V126: "Do you trust your neighborhood?" V128: "Do you trust people you meet for the first time?"* 1 = "trust completely," and 4 = "Do not trust at all."	Same as above
	Nuclear particularized trust	V125: "Do you trust your family?" 1 = "trust completely," and 4 = "Do not trust at all."	Same as above

* This question measures something between generalized trust and extended particularized trust. In the context of the latter, if a person one meets for the first time is introduced by a mutual friend, then he or she should be trusted.

CHAPTER 3

Market Structure in Relation-Based Societies

Salient Features of Relation-Based Market Structure

In general, the market structure in a relation-based society is different from that of a rule-based society. In this chapter, we will discuss some main features of the market structure in relation-based societies and contrast them with those in rule-based societies.

Government and Business

The role of the government in a relation-based society can be summarized as very powerful. As we discussed in the introduction, the fundamental reason why people and businesses try to avoid formal rules and rely on private relationships to conduct business and protect their interest is that the formal rules tend to be opaque and unfair, and the state cannot enforce them impartially. This situation results from the unbalanced power of the state, especially when the executive branch overshadows or controls legislative and judiciary functions. The state controls most lucrative industries, usually in the name of protecting domestic industries or "national security." For instance, the Chinese government explicitly stated in 2006 that it must maintain "absolute control" over the following seven industries: defense, electricity production and distribution, petrochemical, telecommunication, coal, civil aviation, transportation, and shipping.[1] In the same year, official statistics showed that the state-owned enterprises in those controlled industries achieved the highest profit growth in China, accounting for 86% of total profits made by all state-owned enterprises. The raw material and energy industries had about 50% profit growth in the first 5 months of 2006.[2]

Meanwhile, relation-based governments usually give privileges to certain private business people who have close relationships with the government. For example, in Thailand, lucrative industries are tightly controlled by the government and demand "an especially close relationship with 'the centers of power'" to enter.[3] These industries include natural resource extraction, building and engineering contracting, and alcohol distribution and retailing. In general, opportunities are open only to the business people who are well connected with government officials. As analysts observed, there is a key axis of powerful military officials and financiers that dominates the urban political economy in Thailand, and "spectacular success in the growing urban economy was reserved for the small number of business groups that clustered around this axis."[4]

In China, the government has stated that it would allow certain private investors to enter some of the state-controlled industries. The investment must be under state planning and must be qualified as being offered by "high quality private firms."[5] The online comments about this policy suggest that it will give well-connected investors the opportunity to enter these lucrative industries. One commentator said, "This policy is nothing more than creating a few oligarchs who control China's economy. It is to legitimize transferring the lifeline of our national economy to the children of high-ranking officials." Another said, "[Allowing] non-state capital entering the controlled industry? Who has that kind of money to play such a game? Who can win (against the state)? Only the children of the policy makers can play. Only they can win."[6]

A seasoned and very successful entrepreneur in China, Feng Lun, made the following observation about the role of ordinary private businesses under the watchful eyes of the state:

Private businesses in China must realize that they have been and will always be appendices of the state-owned businesses. Thus, the best survival strategies are the following: you can stay far away from the industries in which state-owned firms dominate, being satisfied with your own small plot, contributing actively to philanthropy, and building roads and bridges in your community.

Alternatively, you can partner with the state capital to create a mixed ownership. Leveraging on your professional and managerial ability, you must first preserve the state capital and deliver a good return for it, and then you may gain legitimacy and enjoy a relatively safe environment . . . Facing the state-owned businesses, private businesses must cooperate, not compete; supplement, not replace; follow, not surpass.[7]

In addition to the tight control over many industries by the state, another common feature of market entry barriers in a relation-based society is that while an industry may be formally open to private or foreign investment, the informal barriers, created by the powerful regulatory officials and the exclusive network of incumbents, can be insurmountable. A spokesperson for a national business association in China, Huang Mengfu, complained,

Publicly, some industries appear to be open, but when you try to enter, you will find many hurdles that are so high that it is impossible for you to enter. We call this a "glass door" that is locked. You can look through it, but you can't get in. If you try, you will hit a wall.[8]

A Vietnamese entrepreneur described a similar situation in his country: "It's government policy not to discriminate between the state and private sectors, but in reality the officials who implement the policies often don't treat us equally."[9]

The Tendency to Have More Formal Rules in Relation-Based Societies

Readers who have traveled to relation-based countries, especially to the ones undergoing rapid changes, may observe that compared to rule-based countries, these relation-based countries that are not supposed to closely follow formal public rules actually have *more* formal rules than rule-based countries. Take the case of China, for instance. The formal rules of setting up a limited liability company, the most common form of business organization, are many and complicated. At the turn of the century (late

1990s and early 2000s), I had an experience of setting up a company from scratch and acquiring an existing firm in China. One of the major steps in setting up a new firm was to register it with the local business administration bureau, which first required that a prospective new firm submit a feasibility study (which could be simply rejected by the bureau as "not feasible," a decision we first received), that the owners have valid local resident cards (e.g., Beijing residents may not register a firm in Shanghai), that the company had leased or bought a physical location, and that it deposit the minimally required registered capital in the bank, ranging from 100,000 yuan ($12,000 in 1999) to 30 million yuan ($3.6 million in 1999), depending on the nature of the business and its type of ownership structure. Furthermore, the required cash deposit for the start-up must be verified by the government, which typically charged 0.3% of the total investment as the cost of "performing" the verification. The naming of a start-up was stringently controlled by the state. The format is "location" + "adjective" + "nature of business," for example, "Shen-zhen City Prosperous Fishing Gear." The words "China," "national," "international," or anything that implied a national or international scale were owned by the government; any firms that want to use them must get special permission from the state. (Of course, for someone who has a strong relationship with the authorities and offers them an appealing deal, such words can be part of the company name.) In the case of one company acquiring the other, the regulation is that the acquiring company's registered capital (not the total assets) must be greater than that of the acquired company. If not, even if the acquiring company has enough cash on hand, it cannot buy the other company.

In Vietnam, for example, the state regulation for urban land development involves 22 permits and approvals.[10] Not surprisingly, a feasibility study is required, and it has to be reviewed and approved by two separate agencies. Ultimately, all land development projects must go all the way up to the Vietnamese Prime Minister's Office to get approval! (Imagine if all land development applications had to be approved by the White House in the United States . . .) In Indonesia, even in the post-Suharto (who was very corrupt) era, after substantial changes, the approval procedure for foreign firms to enter "remains lengthy and tedious."[11]

How do we explain the tendency of relation-based governments to set up more formal rules? The reason for this abundance of rules is that the government in a relation-based country is generally more powerful and controls more public and economic resources than its counterparts in rule-based countries. We should keep in mind that the key feature of relation-based societies is not that they lack public rules; it is that the public rules are not fairly made and are not consistently applied. People with close relationships to officials can easily circumvent the rules. In this sense, these stifling rules are evidence of a relation-based system. Researchers commenting about Thailand's complicated business regulation system said this: "The tangle of licensing controls and miscellaneous red tape . . . provided opportunities for the generals to favor their friends."[12] If someone does not have a good connection or refuses to go through private relationships, then doing business in such societies is very difficult. For example, an American developer in Vietnam who did not use private connections or pay bribes spent 5 years to get project approval, 1 year to get a construction permit, and 2 years to get the land use certificates![13]

High Market Entry Barrier

In an economy that relies on private relationship to conduct and protect business activities, business people invest heavily in establishing good relationships with the people who can help them in their business. These people include government officials and established business people. Investment in relationships is "sunk capital" in a sense that once invested, the investor cannot redeem his investment because he cannot resell his established relationship to others.

Private relationships are exclusive, just like a marital or dating relationship, and thus the people who are in a relationship carefully guard it from existing or potential competitors. Any newcomers that try to budge their way into an existing relationship are not welcome.

Thus the market structure of relation-based economies tends to have high entry barriers. In June 2009, I was helping a UK-based telecom group with their market entry strategy in China. I asked the group's marketing executive what their major difficulty in doing business in China was. The executive replied that it was the lack of relationships with the established players in the market. What follows is a typical case of what usually happens to his marketing effort.

> Since I don't know anyone in the major telecom companies in China, I would make cold calls to pitch our services. Well, it is not completely a cold call; I would do my homework on the person I would call and be well prepared. When I call the prospective client, in order to get through to his secretary, I would say that I have an appointment with him. When I get to the target person, he usually asks where I found his name, how I learned about his background, and who introduced me to him. He would first be impressed by my knowledge of him. But once he learned that I was not introduced by anyone, he would say, "come back when you get a proper introduction" and hang up.[14]

In relation-based economies, major industries tend to be dominated by a few insiders. Those insiders are the business people or firms who either are designated players by the government or have close relationships with the government so that they can get special permissions to enter the market. Once they become insiders, they, along with their benefactor—the government regulatory agency—will try to make the entry barrier high so as to protect their (sunk) investment.

In Indonesia, although many sectors appeared to be completely open to foreign investors, few investors would be confident enough to go in solo because the informal barriers were high and complicated. The properly informed foreign investors always went in with a powerful local player, even though such an option was costly due to "fees" or outright corruption. As one researcher noted, experienced foreign investors "knew the value of having a savvy and influential domestic counterpart with good connections who could navigate the still unreformed bureaucracy." The process was so complicated and difficult that it required the Indonesian president's children to help the foreign firms to "sail through this maze."[15]

High Market Exit Barrier

While the reason for high market entry barriers in a relation-based society is easy to understand, why markets in relation-based society have high exit barriers is not so obvious. To understand this, let us examine the entry and exit mechanism of a mafia group—an extremely relation-based organization. To be admitted into a secretive society such as the mafia, the prospective member needs proper introduction from senior members, and he usually needs to complete a difficult, often dangerous, task asked by the organization to show his commitment and loyalty. An example might be obtaining (often through illegal means) valuable artifacts or information, or even killing someone. After a period of informal probation, if he fulfilled his tasks, he will be admitted. At that point, the organization has invested substantial effort and resources in this new member. If a member wants to quit the organization, not only will all the sunk investment in him be lost, but more importantly, he will take many assets with him, such as the secrets of the organization and the connections or networks the organization has given him. In other words, he knows too much to be let go. To deter such damaging behavior, the mafia organization must exterminate quitters, as shown in numerous cases of organized crime.

It is difficult to obtain cases that reveal in detail the cost and difficulty involved in players quitting business relationships, since such relationships are secretive. Nevertheless, we can indirectly assess the difficulty by examining some high-profile cases of exiting a powerful relation-based business network. The late Indonesian president Suharto was a powerful ruler who had forged an extensive and corrupt government-business alliance. When he was forced to step down in 1998 due to the popular uprising, many business people who were closely associated with him or his family suffered great losses in their business ventures.[16] Many of these people invested in these ventures not because the business had cutting-edge technology or superior products or services but because Suharto's power would guarantee an above-market average return no matter what the business did. Similarly, when the powerful businessman turned prime minister of Thailand, Thaksin, fled the country, many of his business associates suffered big losses.[17] Needless to say, the value of their investment in such a relationship was rapidly becoming worthless. And worse yet, some of them may be prosecuted by the new regime on bribery and corruption charges related to the former rulers. We can reasonably conjecture that the business partners of Suharto and Thaksin would do whatever they could to prevent the two from leaving, if they were able.

Business Groups in Relation-Based Markets

Based on our analysis so far, it is no surprise that most successful business people in a relation-based society have cozy relationships with the government. Once a business person has developed a good relationship with the government, it is easy for him to get the entry permission for his chosen industry. In fact, since the relational investment to cultivate a cordial relationship with the government is sunk, he should use the established relationship as much as possible. Thus, instead of entering one industry, the relationship holder may as well enter as many industries as he can. Because most industries are restricted by the government and competition is limited, whoever has the privilege to enter is likely to make money, even though they may not have expertise or experience in the industry.

This logic may partially explain why in relation-based economies there are some huge business groups whose businesses span widely into many unrelated areas. For instance, in Thailand, once well-connected businessmen became successful in a core business, they would use "their privileged access to capital and patronage to extend sideways into related fields. Each had come to dominate a conglomerate of multiple companies."[18] By the late 20th century, some 20 families dominated the urban economy of Thailand. Since they had already established close relationships with the official regulators, they entered many sectors that needed special blessings by the government, and they earned high profits in these restricted businesses.[19] In Indonesia, big conglomerates owned by some prominent families such as the Suharto family were so dominant that the Indonesian people made the expression "It's all in the family" a political joke. One of the largest conglomerates, Salim, had 600 subsidiaries employing 200,000 people in the mid-1990s.[20] In Japan, South Korea, and Hong Kong, the economies are still dominated by big conglomerates (family-owned business groups in Hong Kong, the *keiretsu* in Japan and the *chaebol* in Korea) that are the legacies of the old or passing relation-based system.

Lack of Innovation in Relation-Based Societies

Compared with their counterparts in rule-based economies, firms in relation-based economies lack incentives to adopt new technologies for three main reasons. First, new technology may lead to a faster depreciation of their sunk investment in relations (see chapter 6 for more discussion). Second, in relation-based industries, competition is restrained by incumbent firms and government regulatory agencies. Since new technology tends to stimulate competition, the incumbent relation-based firms tend to be more resistant to adopting new technology. A third reason is that by their nature, established relationships, the main asset of these firms, have the tendency of being backward looking. There is a saying in Chinese that "friendship is like a ceramic vase, the older it is, the better it is." On the contrary, technological innovation is forward looking (see the discussion on similar practice in human resource management in chapter 5).

Trade Flows Between Rule-Based and Relation-Based Countries

If the market entry barrier is higher in relation-based countries, does it affect the trade flows in and out of them? In this section, we examine how the governance environment affects international trade flows, namely, the import (buying) and export (selling) of goods across countries. Essentially, we want to answer the following question:

Which Are Easier to Trade With, Rule-Based or Relation-Based Countries?

Based on our definition, rule-based countries (i.e., representative democracies) are the ones in which public rules (laws and regulations) are fairly made with input from different constituencies and are transparent and universally enforced effectively and efficiently by an impartial state. Thus in the most ideal situation, in rule-based countries, trade rules and regulations tend to be open and equally applied to everyone. Anyone who is interested in conducting international trade can access and study the rules and trade, even if this person is from a relation-based society. Of course, this is the ideal situation; in reality, there are still hidden trade barriers even in rule-based countries. But it is fair to say that in comparison with relation-based countries, the rules of entering rule-based markets are more transparent and thus easier to follow. In relation-based markets, the formal rules are more likely to be just ink on paper, and one must not only know the hidden barriers and the informal rule of the game but also have strong connections with the insiders who control the market entry. Here the concept of "a glass door" is quite appropriate to describe the high entry barrier to a relation-based market. The "magic word" to open the glass door would be one's private connections with the authorities that control the market gate.

Therefore, *everything being equal, it is easier for a relation-based firm to enter a rule-based market to trade than for a rule-based firm to enter a relation-based market.* The reasons are as follows. First, it is difficult for outsiders to have access to the private information about the hidden norms of trade. For them, even getting all the required permits and licenses can be an insurmountable task. Second, due to the weak rule of law in relation-based societies, actually conducting trade is difficult and risky. Compared with domestic trade, international trade requires stronger property rights protection and contract enforcement because of the greater geographic and time separation of delivery and payment. In many relation-based countries, these protections are very weak or even nonexistent. For example, we interviewed a Hong Kong businessman who sold luxury watches to China. He told us that due to the lack of protection for the credit market, he could not ship goods to his distributors in China on credit; he must demand cash payment for his shipment, since the temptation of disappearing with the watches was too high and the legal enforcement was difficult. On the other hand, obviously, it was not very safe to carry a large bag of cash while traveling long distances in China. So he capped his goods delivery at a cash value of about 500,000 yuan ($60,000). (It still sounds very dangerous to carry that much money in cash.) This practice limited the scale of his business.

Trade Flows Between Rule-Based and Relation-Based Countries

There are four types of possible trade relations between rule-based and relation-based countries, as depicted in Figure 3.1: (a) a rule-based country sells (exports) to another rule-based country, (b) a rule-based country exports to a relation-based country, (c) a rule-based country sells to a relation-based country, and (d) a relation-based country exports to another relation-based country.

Let us review each type in turn. The first type, trade between two rule-based countries, is easy in terms of getting through the regulation and market entry. As we discussed earlier, there are some commonalities among all rule-based societies in terms of their political and economic institutions, such as the existence of checks and balances. Furthermore, in order for most people and firms to follow the formal rules and regulations, they must be relatively easy to follow, transparent, and fair. For example, in the United States, import and export do not require any special license or permit (except the restricted items to certain nondemocratic countries that can be used for military purposes). In sum, for an exporter who is familiar with his home country's import and export regulations, learning to navigate in another

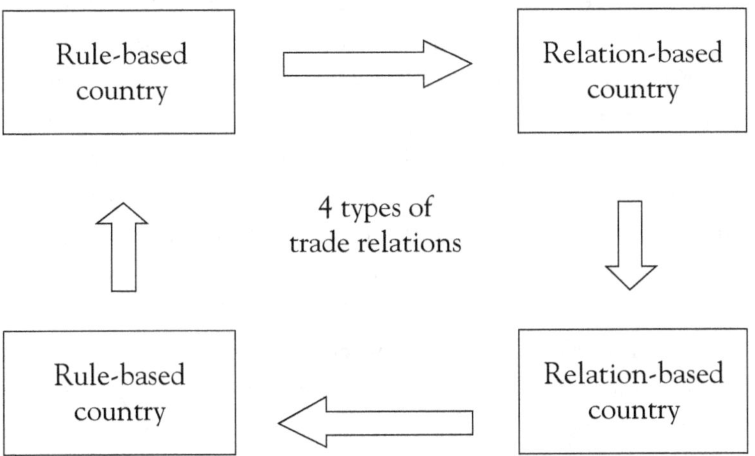

Figure 3.1. Trade patterns between rule-based and relation-based countries

rule-based market should be relatively easy compared to the task of entering a relation-based market.

In the second case, it is much more difficult for an exporter in a rule-based country to sell to a relation-based country. In a relation-based environment, the formal trade rules tend to be very restrictive. For example, in China the right to import and export is strictly controlled by the state. According to export and import laws, it is totally up to the discretion of the state to restrict and require a license on any export or import item. The process of applying for an import or export license is complicated, and qualifications are not automatic. A visit to the official Web site of China's trade regulation agency would reveal a substantial number of products that require a license to import. The official Web site maintains a long list of firms that were punished for violating import or export regulations. The punishment varies from suspending the license for 6 months to revoking the license indefinitely.[21] Similar situations exist in Vietnam, where the state tightly controls international trade, and it is very difficult for ordinary private firms to get a license.[22] In sum, if the foreign seller does not have good relationship with the officials in charge or the powerful players in the industry, it would be very difficult to get in.

In the third case, however, when a firm in a relation-based country exports to a rule-based country, it is more or less on the equal footing with any other firm, including the domestic firms, as far as the regulation and market access are concerned. There is also no additional difficulty imposed specifically on a relation-based firm from outside.

In the last case, in which a firm from a relation-based country sells to another relation-based country, getting through the regulation and gaining market access may not necessarily be easy simply because both are relation-based. While rule-based countries share many similarities in their political and economic institutions, each relation-based country is unique in terms of who has the power to control the private network and how the key players set up the often hidden norms to regulate the insiders. A firm that is very well connected in one relation-based environment may not be able to transfer its connections to a new relation-based country. Thus the trade between two relation-based countries may not necessarily be easy; it is certainly not as easy as trade between two rule-based countries.

The above argument has been confirmed by data. We conducted a statistical analysis to verify the trade pattern in Figure 3.1.[25] We used 44 countries for which we had the Governance Environment Index (GEI) score as the study sample, and for each country we obtained a list of countries it exported to (up to 43 countries) and the volume of the export in U.S. dollars. So in total we have over 1,800 pairs of trading flows among the 44 countries, representing about 90% of world trade. We found the following patterns. First, rule-based countries trade more than relation-based countries. In other words, countries in which laws and regulations are more transparent and fair tend to conduct more international trade. Second, in general, countries with large differences in their governance environments (such as between a highly rule-based country and a highly relation-based country) have low trade flows between them. Third, trade flows between two relation-based countries are also low. Fourth, compared to the trade volume of rule-based countries selling to relation-based countries, the volume of relation-based countries selling to rule-based countries is relatively larger. In sum, all countries like to trade with rule-based countries, while the volume of trade that involves a non-rule-based country tends to be lower.

Policy and Strategic Implications

The policy implication for relation-based countries is that if the government wants to promote trade, it should realize that political and economic reforms that will make the governance environment more rule-based will actually help trade, including both imports and exports.

Exporting firms, especially the ones from rule-based countries, should study not only the prospective partner in a target country but also the governance environment of that country. Understanding the governance environment will help the exporter access the difficulty and risk of entering the country.

Example: The Diamond Market
in the United States and China

The diamond market in the United States and China may provide a good illustration on how the governance environment influences marketing channels and exchanges. Diamonds are small and highly valued, and their quality varies greatly and is difficult to verify. These features make the diamond trade risky—they can be easily stolen or faked. Furthermore, the worldwide supply of diamonds is not only limited but also mostly controlled by one company, De Beers, reinforcing the mystery surrounding the industry.

In 2004 we studied the diamond market in the United States and China to verify our governance environment theory.[24] In the study, we collected data from open sources and also interviewed a diamond merchant in the United States.[25] We also interviewed an official from the diamond industry in China.[26] Below are some of our findings.

Barriers to Entry

In the U.S. diamond industry, the government does not have any special regulations on the diamond industry except the ban on De Beers to directly operate in the United States because it violates U.S. antitrust laws. Nevertheless, U.S. diamond merchants can still legally purchase diamonds from De Beers's selling arm abroad.

In the domestic market, entry is open and the rules are easy to learn. To trade diamonds, one may choose to become a member at the New York Diamond Dealers Club (DDC), which is a trade association that is open to anyone to apply. Its goal is to promote and safeguard a secure, fair, and efficient diamond trade with clearly stipulated rules. The main benefit of being a member is that a trader can expand his business beyond the customers he already knows well, which is the important feature of a rule-based governance system. As legal scholar Lisa Bernstein puts it, the DDC "enables dealers to trade with people about whose reputation they have little information."[27] The DDC is a nongovernment agency that does not have the authority or power to control the industry. One does not have to become a DDC member to be in the diamond business. In fact the diamond merchant we interviewed in the United States is an independent trader whose businesses included cutting, wholesaling, and retailing.

In China, the diamond industry is more regulated than in the United States. There are 12 governmental agencies regulating the diamond trade. According to the Diamond Administration of China (one of the major agencies), a firm had to go through 12 steps in order to enter the trade. The government has also imposed a high tax and fees on the diamond trade. For example, in the early 2000s, the taxes and fees levied on imported rough diamonds reached 40%–50%. The official we interviewed commented that most diamond merchants would not be able to make a profit if they followed all the rules and paid all the taxes and fees. As a result, people who entered and were successful were likely the ones who had good connections with government officials. Thus we can say that *the formal entry barriers are higher in the relation-based environment.*

Channel Exclusivity

The U.S. diamond merchant we interviewed told us that as a wholesaler, he may choose to purchase rough diamonds from any source, and his wholesale status was mostly determined by his business volume and payment history. As a retailer, he was also open to trying out new suppliers and vice versa.

In contrast, exchanges and transactions among Chinese diamond merchants took place mainly "inside the circle" (in the words of our Chinese interviewee). According to him, Chinese diamond merchants tended to avoid dealing with strangers, and they would not sell if the buyer was unknown to them. In general, *relation-based markets are more exclusive.*

Source of Information

In the U.S. diamond market, there are competing sources of publicly available pricing information, such as the *Rapaport Diamond Report.*[28] As we mentioned earlier, verifying the quality of a diamond is complicated and inexperienced buyers can be easily misled. In the United States, authentication is conducted by a third party who is impartial to the prospective transacting parties. The Gemological Institute of America (GIA) is one of the major suppliers of this service. Its mission is "to ensure the public trust in gems and jewelry by upholding the highest standards of integrity, academics, science, and professionalism through education, research, laboratory services, and instrument development."[29] Diamond buyers put a premium on certified diamonds because of the quality and security they provide.

In the Chinese diamond market, timely, accurate, and publicly available pricing sources have yet to be developed. Our official interviewee admitted that it is very difficult for firms to obtain this information in the Chinese market. At the retail level, pricing practice is chaotic. Due to the lack of reliable public information on pricing, consumers do not have much faith in the prices quoted by retailers and the gradation and the uniqueness of each diamond made comparative shopping difficult. A common practice is that retailers first quote an astronomical number, and the prospective buyer replies with a ridiculously low counteroffer, then after intense bargaining the retailer "reluctantly" parts with the diamond for what appears to be a substantial discount from the original quote. According to our interviewee, the industry norm (which is not supposed to be known outside) is to inflate the price by as high as 300%, and then sell at 30% discount. As more and more people have been buying diamonds, China has begun to develop a system of authentication and verification as well. However, our interviewee pointed out a major flaw in the system: The government agency that provides grading certificates is the same agency that set up the technical standards for grading, and it has the authority to designate who can provide grading services. Such a system opens the possibility for insider dealing, compromising the quality of the service. It also encourages local governments to elect trade barriers. For example, the Shanghai authority requires that diamonds sold in Shanghai be graded only by a Shanghai grading agency. Chinese media reported that a considerable number of dishonest merchants, taking advantage of the loophole in the authentication system, sell synthetic diamonds as natural diamonds.[30] This comparison shows that *in a relation-based environment, publicly verifiable and available information for marketing decisions tends to be lacking.*

Trust and Exchange Policies

Trust provides the foundation for diamond merchants to trade efficiently in the United States. As Bernstein succinctly put it, "In the diamond industry, a handshake accompanied by the words *mazel u'broche* creates a binding agreement."[31] One of the major goals of the DDC is to create a trading environment in which trust among dealers is high and trade becomes simple (such as merely mentioning *mazel u'broche*) so that the cost of monitoring the trade is kept at a minimum. Needless to say, the high level of trust is backed by effective and efficient punishment of people who abuse the trust.

Similarly, trust between the consumer and the diamond merchant is also high. The American merchant we interviewed said, "You [the consumer] have to trust [the seller] because you don't know how to grade a diamond. Trust is the first thing and a certificate is the second thing."[32] This high level of trust is backed by a common practice of the 5-day return policy and a variety of options in which the buyer can get the diamond tested and certified by independent agencies and laboratories.

According to our interview, such a high level of trust does not exist in the Chinese diamond industry. Since the majority of diamond transactions at the wholesale level involve smuggling or tax evasion, merchants keep their activities secretive at all costs. Throughout the interview, the Chinese official mentioned repeatedly that it was the state's predatory policy that forced the merchants to circumvent the laws and regulations: "They must do so to survive." Unlike their counterpart in the United States, Chinese retail merchants did not offer any return or exchange policy. When asked why, the official replied that it was commonly believed in China that the consumers would abuse the policy (such as switch and return) and the costs would be too high to support it. Thus we conclude that *marketers in relation-based governance environments are less likely to adopt practices, such as generous return or exchange policies, that are based on generalized trust.*

Dispute Resolutions

In the diamond trade, due to the unique features of diamonds—small in size, high in value, and its quality and value difficult to evaluate with the naked eye—disputes are frequent and often involve substantial value.

Even in the United States, these unique features make the use of the legal system to resolve diamond trade disputes less desired for two reasons. First, the court process is too slow. Diamond disputes usually involve large value and the disputing merchants cannot afford to have such big amounts of capital frozen for years pending a court ruling. Second, the reputation cost is high, since once going to court it will become public. To solve these issues, the DDC has developed a dispute resolution system that is not only relied upon by members but also preferred by nonmembers of the system. The DDC arbitration is closed door, fair, and fast. The rules of DDC arbitration are public and transparent, and they are strictly enforced. It also has a mechanism of checks and balances by outside forces: If a disputing party feels that the arbitration is tainted by some irregularities, he or she may ask a New York state court to review the case under New York law. In this sense, the DDC arbitration is a typical public ordering system that satisfies all the major requirements to be an effective and efficient rule-based system: Rules are clearly written and publicly available, and enforcement is impartial, strict, and fast.

Through public sources, we found little information about how disputes were resolved in China's diamond industry. The Chinese official we interviewed made the following observation when asked about dispute resolution in China's diamond industry:

> Not rule-based. Almost all rough diamonds in China are black trade or gray trade, with black being smuggling and completely illegal, and gray being tax evading. Thus firms face great risks in their operations, for if one party cheats, the other party cannot resort to public ordering to make a complaint . . . Disputes are usually resolved between the two involved parties, without a third party. If one is dishonest, the other party incurs a loss . . . This has been one of the biggest problems in this industry . . . The victim does not dare to come forward.

Thus we conclude that *when disputes arise in a market exchange, the involved parties tend to rely on themselves to resolve them in a relation-based environment, while in a rule-based environment, people are more likely to resort to a third party to solve them.*

So, what are the implications for firms that are doing or plan to do business in a relation-based society? I am sure readers are asking this question, and I am also sure that many readers can come to some insightful conclusions as to the implications based on their knowledge and experience. In the concluding chapter of the book, we will discuss business implications in detail.

CHAPTER 4

How Much Do We Trust Disclosed Information?

Investment Protection in Relation-Based Markets

In the late 1990s, at a conference on how to invest in China, a senior analyst from Hong Kong lamenting the poor quality of information disclosure among the listed firms in China joked that "reading the annual reports of the Chinese companies is like going to a bikini fashion show—what you see is interesting, but what you don't see is vital!"

While it is well known that accurate financial information is vital for making investment decisions (such as purchasing shares of a company), what is less known is how people protect their investment when publicly disclosed information is not trustworthy. In this chapter, we will discuss information and investment protection under different governance environments.

Earnings Management in Relation-Based Societies

Earnings management is a managerial accounting practice that manipulates earnings information by either making it appear higher or lower on the books. A firm's income fluctuates from time to time. The manager of a firm may want to smooth the earnings report over time by using certain accounting measures. For example, if the manager wants to make the earnings look high, he can keep uncollectable (losses) as accounts receivable for a longer period than usual. On the other hand, if he wants to hide profits for "rainy days" or other purposes, then he may set aside a greater amount of reserve for uncollectable accounts. In addition to these practices, which may still be within the legal limit, the manager may also use outright illegal means to manipulate the accounting information, such as what the managers of the now defunct Enron and WorldCom did to mislead their investors.

Indeed, the incentives for earnings management exist for firms in both rule-based and relation-based economies. However, the practice is more prevalent for firms in relation-based countries. One of the reasons for this disparity is government policy in relation-based societies. As we discussed in the introduction, a relation-based political regime is usually authoritarian (or totalitarian) and suppresses opposition and undermines the checks and balances in the political system (if these checks and balances exist at all). This high level of concentration of power usually leads to more abuse of power, which prompts the relation-based government to keep its operations secret. A free press, which spurs competition among the media to publish newsworthy information, would be more likely to expose the corruptions and abuses by the regime. Thus it is necessary for the relation-based government to control the flow of information in the society, a practice that can be called "information manipulation" to parallel earnings manipulation at the firm level.

Information Management by a Relation-Based Government

An example of information management by a relation-based government is the Chinese government's long history of manipulating public information, going back to Mao Zedong's era. Mao Zedong ruled China from 1949 to 1976 with a radical communist ideology and totalitarian control over the society. Mao ignored the legal rules he set up and believed that the end justified the means. It was reported that when U. S. President Richard Nixon visited him in 1972, Mao told Nixon, "I don't obey any laws!"[1] Even Nixon, who did not have much respect for the law either, was shocked. Mao manipulated public information for his benefit. Perhaps the largest information manipulation was the concealment of the great famine from 1959 to 1962, during which tens of millions died of starvation. Even today, the Chinese Communist Party refuses to tell the world how many died in the famine. Estimates run from 27 million to over 40 million.[2]

Another example of information management in relation-based societies is the government's alteration of photos to manipulate public opinions. During the Soviet era, Joseph Stalin, the Communist Party head, doctored photos based on the relationship he had with other leaders in the photo. When someone lost his favor, this person would be removed from the picture. Like Stalin, Mao manipulated who should be retained or wiped out from photos taken with other comrades depending on who was in favor with Mao at any given time. Even today, the Chinese Communist Party still practices this technique.[3]

Local officials in China routinely manipulate economic statistics to serve their agendas: If an official wants to get promoted, he makes the numbers such as the economic growth rate larger; if he wants to get aid, he shrinks the numbers. This practice is jokingly referred to in China as "officials make numbers, numbers make officials."

Not only does the government suppresses or invent news, it also schedules major, newsworthy projects and chooses when to release the major positive news. Major government-sponsored projects, such as nuclear weapon tests and the space program (e.g., launching a satellite), must be timed to gain the highest impact or to distract the public from major negative news. For instance, in September 2008, a major scandal was exposed in which leading dairy companies in China sold melamine-tainted milk that made tens of thousands of babies sick and caused several deaths. The Chinese government then announced that it would move a space shuttle launch earlier than originally scheduled. Critics suspected that the government used the shuttle launch and the space walk to steer the world's attention away from the tainted-milk scandal.[4]

As a result of public information management by the government, people in China have not had much faith in official news or statistics. Public information in general is less trustworthy in relation-based societies, and people living in these societies are always seeking reliable information from informal channels, such as rumors and hearsay.

Information Management by Firms

In an environment where the government manipulates public information, there is very little reason why firms should not do the same to their advantage, so they mimic what the government does and manipulate their operating information. According to our interviews with accountants in China, it is common for firms to manipulate their earnings reports.

Private firms tend to lower earnings to avoid taxes. Studies show that tax evasion by firms in China is widespread. Large losses tend to trigger auditing by the tax authorities, so the firms that manipulate earnings in order to avoid taxes only show a small loss.

Managers of state-owned firms report more earnings to get promoted or to simply keep their jobs. In their study of executive compensation and firm performance in China, economists Kato and Long found that "Chinese executives [of state-owned firms] are penalized for making negative profits."[5] But they also found that the executives are not further rewarded for profits that are much greater than zero. Their study confirms the existence of a very strong incentive for Chinese state firm executives to engage in earnings management to bring the profit rate into positive territory. But there is also no further incentive to push profits higher.

These two tendencies suggest that firms in China tend to manipulate their profit rate close to zero. To verify this, my colleagues and I did a simple statistical analysis: We created a distribution of all manufacturing firms in China by their profit level as measured by return on assets (ROA),[6] as shown in Figure 4.1.

In Figure 4.1, the tallest curve is the ROA distribution of Chinese firms, the second tallest curve is the ROA distribution of U.S. firms, whereas the most flat curve is a hypothetical normal distribution curve in the absence of earnings management.

Compared to the ROA distribution of U.S. firms, Chinese firms show a much greater spike around zero on the positive side, which is a strong indication that Chinese firms adjust their ROA to a slightly positive value.

While the purpose of earnings management in China may be tax evasion or promotion seeking, a serious unintended consequence results. Outsiders cannot rely on a firm's financial report to accurately evaluate the firm, which means that outsiders may not be willing to invest in the firm. This deterrent explains why relation-based firms tend to rely on internal and informal financing.

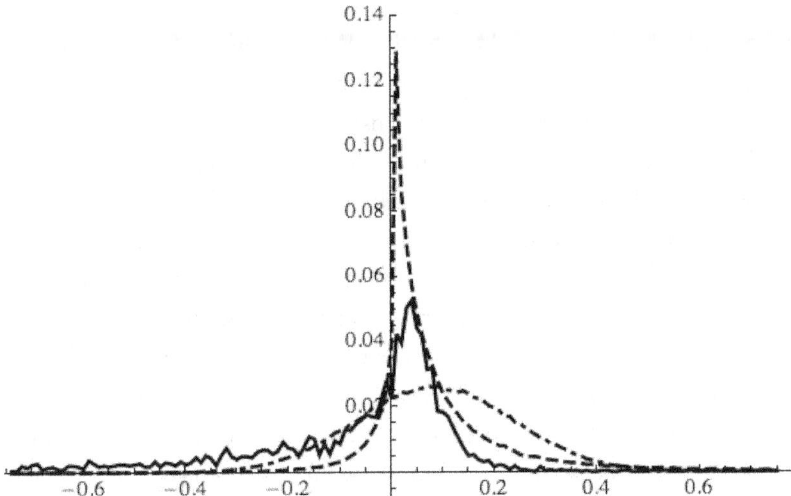

Figure 4.1. Distributions of return on assets in China, the United States, and normal distribution

Note: China = long dotted line; United States = solid line; normal distribution = short dotted line.

Source: Li, et al. (2008).

Relation-Based Ways of Financing

According to research, the Chinese business community in Thailand relies primarily on informal means to raise capital for their business expansion.[7] The most common way to raise capital is the *chae*, which is a rotating credit society in which all members contribute and each member takes his turn to borrow a sum contributed by all members. The key to the functioning of this credit society is careful screening and admitting members who have a good reputation and are trustworthy. Another way to finance their business is to engage in discounting postdated checks, which means to cash a check with a future date with a discount. The risk of receiving a bad check is reduced by the community's ability to verify and monitor borrower's business and credit. A third way to raise capital is an equity joint venture in which the fund provider will invest in the fund seeker's project. All the above financing methods require efficient and accurate monitoring mechanisms that can verify the prospective fund seeker's credit worthiness (*ex ante* monitoring), his ability to perform his duty (interim monitoring), and where his assets are in case he fails to deliver (*ex post* monitoring). If the parties involved are outsiders, such as banks, then this kind of monitoring mechanism would be almost impossible to use, or the cost of doing so would be too high to make business sense.

In such an environment, formal credit risk management does not work efficiently and banks often incur high losses from bad loans. For example, in China, nearly 50% of bank loans to small borrowers cannot be collected, whereas loans arranged privately using the above monitoring mechanism seldom go bad.[8] As a result, banks charge a very high transaction fee and interest to compensate for the risk associated with the difficulty of evaluating credit in a relation-based market. As commented by a researcher who studied Vietnam's real estate market, getting loans from banks "was the most expensive option" to finance a project.[9]

Why Foreign Investment Flows to Countries With Poor Legal Systems

In relation-based economies that lack publicly reliable information and effective and efficient public ordering to protect investment, how do foreign investors enter those markets and protect their investment?

The inflows of foreign investment across countries have some interesting patterns, which, as one would expect, are influenced by the governance environment, namely, how investments are protected in a country. Researchers have studied this issue extensively and have accumulated a great deal of knowledge about how a country's legal system affects the inflow of foreign investment. In general, they have found that a poor legal system deters foreign investment. This finding is hardly surprising: Intuition would tell us that if the legal system does not offer effective and efficient protection of property rights, investors will be reluctant to invest.

However, this argument fails to explain why countries with a poor legal system attract sizable foreign investment. Take the case of China, its legal system is controlled by a single party—the Chinese Communist Party—and judges are political appointees that tend to be corrupt. Despite this, China has been attracting huge amounts of foreign investment.

Of course, one may argue that the huge market in China provides great opportunities for production and consumption. While this is certainly a major factor in attracting foreign investment to China, it does not address the issue of how investment is protected in countries like China, where the rule of law is weak. In order to understand better this question, we need to distinguish two types of foreign investment: direct and indirect investment.

Direct Investment and Indirect (Portfolio) Investment

Capital investment, including both foreign investment and domestic investment, can be classified into two types: direct and indirect. Direct investment refers to an arrangement in which the investor *invests and controls* (*manages*) the project or entity in which he or she invests. This is usually the case when the investor invests a large share of the total investment and thus controls the investment. The investor can access all the information about the investment, manage it, and make all the decisions about it. An example of direct investment would be someone investing to build and operate a restaurant or a garment factory.

Indirect investment refers to the type of investment in which the investor *cannot directly control* (*manage*) the investment. Usually the investment accounts for a small percentage of the total investment so that the investor cannot directly exercise his control right or management right. In this case, the investor becomes a passive investor; he does not have firsthand, unlimited access to information relative to the investment such as the accounting books or board meeting minutes. He has access to information about the state of the operation he has investment in through annual reports and shareholders meetings. An example of indirect investment would be buying a few shares of stock in a large company such as AT&T. In general, indirect investments include securities offered in the public market, such as stocks or bonds of publicly listed companies. This kind of investment is commonly referred to as "portfolio investment." We will use "indirect investment" and "portfolio investment" interchangeably in this book.

When we break down the total foreign investment that flows into China, we find an unbalanced distribution. Most investment is direct investment, and portfolio investment accounts for a small proportion. In the 3-year period from 2004 to 2006, China received a net of $181 billion foreign direct investment (FDI) and a net of –$53 billion foreign portfolio investment (FPI). In the same period, the United States received a net of –$71 billion FDI and $1.9 trillion FPI. (Interestingly, most of the foreign portfolio investment in the United States is sent by the Chinese government and other Chinese investors. Obviously, China has faith in the public financial market of the United States.) The popular view that China is the largest recipient of foreign investment is not correct. It is only correct in terms of foreign direct investment. In terms of total foreign investment, the United States is still by far the largest.

Types of Investment and Modes of Governance

The two types of investment require different governance mechanisms for protection.[10] In portfolio investments, since the investors do not have direct access to operational and managerial information or direct control over the managers, they must rely on *publicly* available information, such as annual reports or company press releases, to aid their investment decisions. For the portfolio investors, the timeliness and accuracy of the public information is vital. If disputes arise between the investors and the management of the investment, they usually resort to public rules, through the courts, to resolve them. The court must rely on publicly verifiable information to make a ruling.

In sum, *portfolio investment requires a rule-based governance environment for effective and efficient protection.* An anecdote about information distortion and stock price manipulation in China may illustrate this point. In the late 1990s, there was a listed company called Tiange Technology whose products included freshwater snapping turtle, a delicacy in China. In order to manipulate its stock price, management would issue statements such as "due to a flood, our turtles were washed away" to drive the price down; if it wanted to boost the price, it would issue something like "the flood receded and our turtles swam back."[11]

When I taught this topic in my international business class, I always asked my students, "What information would you rely on and where would you get it when you evaluate whether to buy a listed company's stock?" Most American students would start with "studying the prospective company's annual report and quarterly filings." My students in Asia, on the other hand, would suggest ways such as "talk with someone with inside information" or "follow someone who is in the know." In a class in Taiwan, a student said, "Follow A-Chen!" Seeing that I was totally lost, he explained that A-Chen was the nickname for Wu Shu-chen, wife of the former president of Taiwan, Chen Shui-bian, who was charged for corruption. His wife is known for her "ability" to always pick the winning stocks. When I pressed my Asian students further with the question, "What about studying the annual report?" they would always dismiss it by saying, "Most companies cook the numbers. So who would trust their annual reports?"

As for direct investment, there is no separation between investors and management. The investors are the insiders who are also directly involved in managing the investment and share the information about the investment *privately* among themselves, which substantially reduces the information gap between the investors and the management that exists in portfolio investment. The direct control by owners in direct investment makes it easier for the owners to protect their assets *privately* than that to protect portfolio investments. In other words, the need for an effective and efficient legal system to protect the investment is not as high for direct investment as for indirect investment.

Now let us consider the type of investment and mode of governance together. Based on the above analysis, we may conjecture that in rule-based societies, foreign investment tends to be in the form of portfolio investment, whereas in the relation-based societies, foreign investment should be in the form of direct investment. Is this pattern supported by evidence? We need to examine the relationship between the mode of governance and the type of investment using data.

If we compare the combination of FDI and FPI in three of the least rule-based countries—China, Azerbaijan, and Pakistan—with three of the most rule-based countries—the United States, Australia, and the Netherlands—we get the following numbers: During the 3-year period from 2004 to 2006, the relation-based group attracted $63 billion FDI per annum, while losing $16 billion in FPI yearly, whereas the rule-based group incurred a loss of $64 billion in FDI, while gaining $701 billion in FPI annually. This pattern suggests that when investors invest in relation-based countries, they prefer direct investment. In order to further confirm this, I plotted foreign direct investment over total foreign investment against the Governance Environment Index (GEI), which was introduced in chapter 2. The pattern is quite clear: The less a country is rule-based, the higher the proportion of the total foreign investment that is direct investment. When foreign investors invest in countries with poor legal systems and unreliable public financial information, they tend to choose direct investment over indirect investment.[12]

Figure 4.2 shows that the less a country is rule-based, the greater the proportion of foreign investment is direct investment.

This finding helps us to better understand why China attracted so much foreign direct investment and relatively little portfolio investment. Foreign investors choose direct investment in China *because of*, rather than *despite*, the absence of the rule-based governance environment.

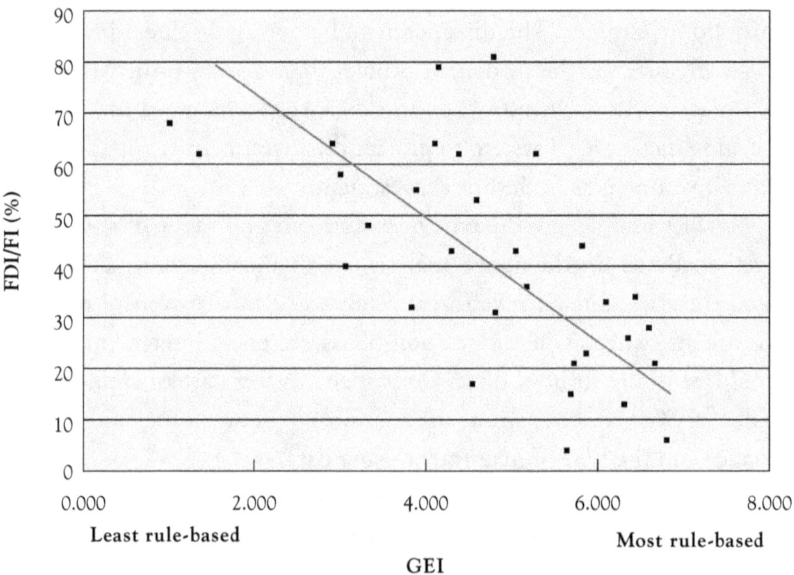

Figure 4.2. Governance environment and foreign investment

Note: The horizontal axis is the score of GEI, which has been adjusted to a scale of 0 (least rule-based) to 8 (most rule-based). The vertical axis is the proportion of foreign direct investment in the total foreign investment in a country: FDI/FI = (foreign direct investment)/(total foreign investment). Each dot in the chart represents a country.

Source: Li (2005).

When public ordering is not effective and efficient, direct investment gives them more control and thus better protection through private relationships. This finding also explains why in some of the least rule-based countries, such as Rwanda, Kyrgyzstan, or Armenia, some 99% of foreign investments were in direct investment, whereas the percentage was substantially lower in rule-based countries such as the United States (23%) or Finland (6%).[13]

Implications of Investment Type and Governance Mode

The above discussion on investment type and governance mode has several implications. First, investors must study a country's governance environment before deciding whether to invest there and what mode of investment is optimal for the protection of the investment. Second, due to the low quality of public financial information, the risk of investing in the public financial market, such as the stock market, is higher. Following the same logic, due to the fact that firm's accounting information is less reliable (as reflected in the high level of earnings management in Chinese firms), outside investors are reluctant to invest in relation-based firms. These facts suggest that the capital market is limited mostly to relational investment, and the cost of capital in the public capital market is higher in a relation-based economy.

The complexity of property rights differs from industry to industry. In general, the property right structure is relatively simple in manufacturing industries, such as the shoe and the garment industries, where the quality and quantity of the products are easy to verify and thus workers and manufacturers can be paid on a regular basis. Logically, the protection of property rights and investments in those industries is relatively straightforward. On the other hand, in the financial industry, the property right structure can be very complex, such as in initial public offerings of stocks, options, and other complex financial deals. For those products and services, the property rights protection is complicated and requires strong legal protection, which is better in rule-based societies. Thus, in general, for investors who are evaluating different industries in which to invest in a relation-based market, if everything else is equal, the investors should favor industries that have simpler property right structures.

CHAPTER 5

Mafia Boss or Modern Manager?

Management and Working Relationships in Relation-Based Firms

In the heyday of the economic opening up in China in the 1980s and 1990s, the name Yu Zuomin was a household word. Mr. Yu was the head of the famous village enterprise called Daqiuzhuang, a village of some 4,000 people that had operated a booming conglomerate of steel, piping, printing, electronics, and related upstream and downstream businesses since the start of the economic reform in 1978. By 1990, Daqiuzhuang had achieved a per capita income of $3,400, 10 times greater than China's average. Its success had earned it titles such as "the richest village in China" and "China's first village."

A main success factor of Yu and his Daqiuzhuang was that Yu was an expert in cultivating cordial private relationships with key government officials who, in turn, gave him inside information on government policies and granted many tax favors to Daqiuzhuang, giving it a huge advantage in the marketplace. Without Yu's ability to obtain these tips and concessions from the government, Daqiuzhuang would not have been as successful. So when Yu was asked about the ownership of the more than 1 billion yuan assets (about $130 million) of the village, which on paper was owned collectively by the whole village, Yu answered, "You can say that it is mine."[1]

Internally, Yu's management style was equally impressive. He commanded absolute authority. "We must follow him with no questions asked," villagers said when they were interviewed. His famous slogan in hiring senior managers was, "You may have your own ideas, as long as they are the same as mine. If not, you know who has to go." He appointed his family members and relatives as his lieutenants. But he also used people who were not related to him. In fact, the manager who played the second most important role in Daquizhuang's development was Mr. Liu, a non-family member recruited by Yu against some opposition in the village. The way Yu controlled his managers and employees was through requiring everyone to be unconditionally loyal to him and him only.

The downfall of Daqiuzhuang appeared accidental and yet fateful: It all started with the death of a general manager of one of the subsidiaries. Like Yu, the deceased general manager used to run his subsidiary as a dukedom, and he was the only one who controlled all the vital information. So his sudden death virtually paralyzed the subsidiary. No one knew where the real accounting books were or who had loaned to or borrowed from the subsidiary. All of this information went to the grave with the deceased manager.

Yu was upset and began to persecute the associates of the deceased manager. He illegally arrested them and tortured them. One of them was beaten to death by Yu's associates. When the government heard this, it sent police to the village to investigate. Yu asked the suspected associates to go into hiding, ordered all the villagers to barricade the village, and waged a war against the police. Yu was subsequently arrested by the government in 1993 and given a 20-year sentence. He died in 1999. Ten years later, many villages in Daqiuzhuang still view him as a great leader who brought them out of poverty, not a criminal.[2]

Is Yu a mafia boss or a business CEO?

The Relation-Based Organization Structure and Management Style

Organizational Structure

In a multicountry study of management style, author Shimoni observed that the Swedish manager he studied seems to delegate more, whereas Thai managers centralize their power.[3] The author did not use the rule-versus relation-based framework to explain the results, but we know from chapter 2 that Sweden is a rule-based society and Thailand is relation-based. In our leadership and management survey, we found that

American managers delegate more than their counterparts in China,[4] and we also know that the former is more rule-based than the latter.

Relation-based firms tend to have the following characteristics in organizational structure: They tend to be highly centralized, the head of the firm tends to exert absolute power, and the boss is less likely to delegate authority to his or her managers. The reason is that the head manages his or her firm by using his or her private connections to deal with external relationships, such as with customers and suppliers in the market or the government. These relationships are secretive (to prevent from his competitors intercepting them) and personal, and the information he relies on to make decisions tends to be private and unquantifiable (such as who is playing golf with whom). Thus it is difficult to delegate those tasks to subordinates.[5]

Private Relations Are Hard to Transfer

This pattern was obvious in our field research in China. In a rule-based environment, CEOs use a secretary to answer telephone calls and make appointments. In China, many CEOs we interviewed did not use such a systematic way to handle communications and appointments. Some of them answered phone calls and made appointments themselves. Another interesting observation in China was that some executives would have several telephone sets on their desk, and the executive would be busy answering them. A similar pattern was seen among Vietnamese executives.[6] Each of those phones was dedicated to a special relationship.

At first we were puzzled by this: Labor cost is much lower in China; so if a CEO in the United States can afford to hire one secretary, then a Chinese CEO of equal status should be able to hire five. Why do they handle these calls themselves? The answer is that a private relationship is not transferable. The boss cannot use subordinates to handle his important relationships. First, doing so may offend the other party ("Why doesn't your boss call me personally?"). Second, there may be sensitive information between them, and the relationship is too subtle for the subordinate to handle. For example, sometimes we did reach a subordinate of the big boss, but the subordinate would not know how to reply to our calls since he or she did not know what the relationship between us and the boss was.

This fact brings up another point about handling relationships in a relation-based environment. During my research in China, I often contacted a CEO friend of mine and asked him to have lunch so that I could exchange management ideas with him. Usually, he would say yes to the lunch but would not commit to a firm date. If I pushed for a date, he would say, "We will see" without a definite date. And without any warning, he would call me at 11:00 a.m. and say, "Shaomin, let's have lunch at 12. I will send a car to pick you up."

This is typical relation-based relationship management. My CEO friend needs to leave his calendar open for more important relationships, such as with government officials, who dictate when to meet the CEO. Having lunch with me, a professor friend, is fun, but should not jeopardize his opportunity to meet his official friends because they are vital to his business. In the early 1990s, when the chairman of J. P. Morgan went to meet the party chief of the city of Tianjin in China with a confirmed appointment made in advance, the party chief was not there to receive him! The party chief's aide just told the chairman matter-of-factly, "By the way, the party chief is not available today."[7] One can only guess that the party chief must have a more important relationship to take care of. Like the way my CEO friend treated me, appointments tend to be more fluid in a relation-based society.

Titles Don't Tell All

Deng Xiaoping, the late paramount leader of China, had no official title in the Chinese government or in the Communist Party, but the chairman of the central government, the state premier, and all the politburo members reported to him. When a researcher asked a business leader in Vietnam about his role in one of the companies he was associated with, he replied that he was "an unofficial vice-director."[8] It is interesting that his role is informal and yet so precise.

In a relation-based firm, the formal title may not accurately reflect the importance or power of an employee. For example, as shown in Figure 5.1, in a relation-based firm, the CEO's secretary may have greater influence on the CEO than his lieutenants, because he or she may know more private information about the CEO, and the CEO may trust him or her

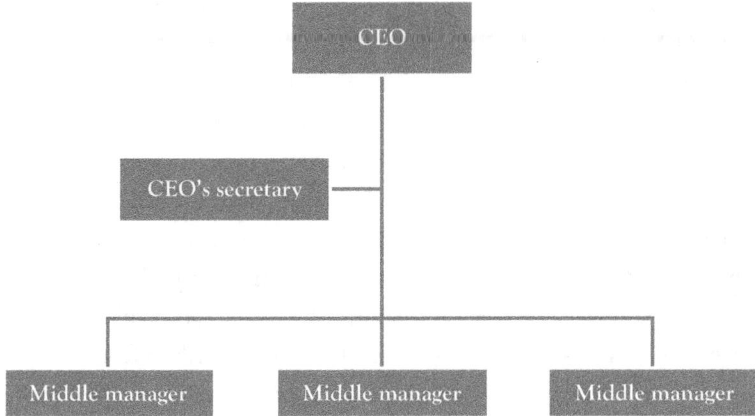

Figure 5.1. A typical organization chart

more.[9] In general, the closer one is to the center of the power, the greater the access to that power and the greater one's influence and position in the organization. During our study of management style in China, we found that in a number of firms, the CEO's secretary was very powerful.[10]

Relation-based bosses tend to bypass the middle managers to reach the rank-and-file employees directly. In our study of a telecom company in China, we found that the CEO maintained such great power distance that she required all employees to address her as "madam." The way she managed the company was to use the rank-and-file employees as informants to report on their immediate supervisors, and she would in turn use these reports to reward or punish her mid-level managers. Since the middle management was kept in the dark about her intention and policy, they had great fear of her and were constantly guessing and betting on her next move.

Formal Rules in Relation-Based Organizations

It would be a mistake to think that relation-based firms do not have many formal rules. Our research indicates that more often than not, relation-based firms have more formal rules and regulations. However, these rules do not apply to the boss. Our management and leadership survey, conducted in both the United States and China, showed that, compared to the U.S. respondents, a significantly higher percentage of

Chinese respondents agreed that "the employees are constantly being checked on for rule violations," and more Chinese respondents agree that "orders and communications are often made in written form."[11] These results are also confirmed by an in-depth interview we conducted in an American-invested firm operating in Shenzhen, China. The human resource director of the firm told us that the firm introduced a set of new regulations intended to increase the fringe benefit for the employees. And to his surprise, many employees looked at the new policy with suspicion and few used it. The reason behind this suspicion is that due to the legacy of a relation-based environment in which firms use formal rules as a tool to constrain workers and not the upper management, employees tend to view any rules categorically negatively.[12] We will further discuss under what conditions relation-based firms tend to erect more formal rules when we discuss the transition of relation-based firms in chapter 8.

Lack of Strategic Planning

Our study also revealed that relation-based firms usually lack formal strategic planning. Formal strategic planning requires systematically making strategic choices based on information that is derived from collecting and analyzing codified or quantified data about markets, the competition, and internal operations using statistical models.

Unfortunately, such information is rare in relation-based markets. Annette Kim, who studied the Vietnamese real estate development market, noted that there is an "absence of updated, publicly accessible land use plans, land registration records, industry reports, and comprehensive market studies, reliable information is difficult to obtain."[13]

As a result, in relation-based firms, most competitive intelligence is privately stored and processed in the head of the boss. Such information tends to be nonquantifiable and kept secret by the boss and is therefore not suitable for systematical analysis to aid formal strategic management.[14] As Kim wrote about the Vietnamese real estate market, "I found that [the real estate firms] were quite secretive about the way they found land sites. They refused to explain how they found land."[15]

Human Resource Management Practices

The way symphony orchestras recruit music instrument players can perhaps best illustrate the differences between rule-based and relation-based hiring practice. In the United States, most of the professional orchestras use "blind" auditions in their hiring process, in which the candidates sit behind a screen and play, and he or she cannot make any sound that could potentially reveal his or her identity, such as speaking or coughing. Even the candidate's footsteps must be muffled by a rug. The only information that the examiners can use to judge the player is the playing.

In China, it used to be the case that no symphony orchestra used blind auditions. Now, many still don't use it. When I asked a Chinese musician who used to play in an orchestra in China why they did not use it, he told me that the examiners needed to know with whom the candidate studied, among other reasons.[16]

The above example and the discussion in the next section "No Exit, No Voice" show that having the right relationship is far more important than professional qualifications in hiring in a relation-based environment. A relationship is one of the rare goods that the older it is, the better it is. This is why we often hear someone boasting that he has known a certain powerful person, such as the president or a CEO, since childhood. Hiring based on relationships is a backward-looking philosophy. The employer pays more attention to the past of the prospective employee, making sure he or she has a good reputation in his or her circle. This kind of hiring philosophy is not conducive to taking initiative and making innovation in work, which involves the risk of failure and therefore of damaging one's established relationships or reputation. For example, studies on the Thai culture noted that this philosophy does not encourage Thais to take initiative in organizations.[17]

On the contrary, in a rule-based environment, which, compared to the relation-based hiring philosophy, is more forward looking, firms tend to seek new employees who show good potential for future achievement.

No Exit, No Voice

Having been an executive in both the United States and China gave me the opportunity to observe the supervisor-subordinate relationship firsthand in the two different environments. And being a researcher enables me to make sense out of the patterns I observed. Sitting in a joint business meeting between an American firm and a Chinese firm is quite interesting. On the American side, everyone would compete to speak up so that they wouldn't be mistaken as timid or shy. And you cannot easily spot who the boss is. On the Chinese side, you can immediately identify who the boss is—he is the one who speaks, while his subordinates sit there in silence. The subordinates only talk when the boss asks them to fill in some details such as a sales figures. (One of my interviewees told me that firms in China are reluctant to hire graduates from Peking University, the most elite school in China, because as rookie members in a firm, instead of sitting quietly in meetings, these graduates would give a summary speech after the boss talked!)

Similar patterns exist in other relation-based societies. Researchers of expatriate manager-local employee relationships found that "Thais have interesting ideas, but may not voice them if the expatriates have presented different ideas."[18]

Why don't, or shouldn't, subordinates in relation-based firms speak up in meetings, while their counterparts in rule-based firms compete to offer their opinions in front of their superior?

One of the reasons, I would argue, is the structure of the job market. As we discussed in the preceding section, in a rule-based job market, the hiring process is more transparent, impersonal, and merit based. Job applicants are hired based on their education credentials and abilities. Once hired, the subordinate should show his or her worth by offering his or her knowledge and opinions, which hopefully are new to the boss, and they may even be different from the boss's view. If what they offer is not appreciated by the boss, they should go back to the job market and look for another place where their opinions are more valued.

In a relation-based job market, connections are vitally important. As the cliché goes, "It is not what you know, but *who* you know." A PhD student in our school, who is from China, told me a story that a classmate of hers, who was a below-average student, got a lucrative financial analyst job that had attracted many highly competent applicants. Her classmate just mentioned that her uncle was the CEO of another big bank, and she was hired right on the spot. In such a job market, firms tend to connect to each other and there is an informal guild that controls the market. It is often the case that one needs his or her boss's blessing to find another job.[19] Thus, if someone speaks up in a meeting in a way that offends his or her boss, it would be difficult for this person to find another job in the market. Without the exit option, employees must be extremely careful when voicing their opinions.

When Rules Meet Relations in the Workplace: The Frictions Between the Two Systems

Talent Flows Between Rule-Based and Relation-Based Societies

Logically, rule-based and relation-based environments attract different types of talents. Here, a personal observation may help illustrate this point. As a Chinese student studying in the United States, I got to know many people with a similar background: coming from a relation-based society to study in a rule-based society. So when they finished their study, they all faced a choice: stay in the United States, or go back to China?

My general observation is that people who have good connections in China or are good at networking and cultivating private relations are more likely to go back to China, and the ones who focus on their specialized knowledge tend to stay in the United States. When I was working at AT&T, I recruited a Chinese man who had just received his PhD in statistics from a prestigious university in the northeastern region of the United States. He is highly intelligent and specializes in mathematics and statistics, and he does not like the Chinese way of getting ahead using private connections. He has excelled at AT&T. Recently, at a gathering, he told me that he was so glad that he did not go back to China because building personal connections was just not his "cup of tea." Of course, the reader should be cautioned that this is just my observation, not a scientific study.

The Expatriate Failure Issue

In international business operations, one of the major challenges for multinational corporations is how the managers sent from the headquarters manage their foreign subsidiaries effectively and efficiently. Many studies show that these expatriate managers—managers working in a foreign country—have a high failure rate.[20] Sending expatriates to manage foreign subsidiaries is expensive. The total package of sending a manager abroad for a multinational corporation is usually three times the manager's cost back home. Thus, when an expatriate manager fails to complete his or her assignment, it will cost more for the company since there are sunk costs of sending the failed manager to the foreign post, such as training, learning, and relocation.[21]

Existing research on expatriate failure has identified the lack of understanding of or the inability to adopt the local culture as the major reason of failure. As a remedy, this stream of research has suggested using cross-cultural training with the prospective expatriate managers. While these cross-culture training efforts may help, they tend to cover mostly cultural norms, such as the "do's and don'ts" in a specific culture, for example, presenting your business card with two hands instead of one.

In the early 1990s, when I hosted a Chinese business delegation at AT&T, the head of the delegation, who was the president of a state-owned company in China, would wave his middle finger to make a point in meetings. Naturally, this gesture startled the American attendees in the meeting, but we all realized that his gesture was innocent and due to years of isolation in China, he was not aware of the meaning of waving the middle finger in America. At the end of his visit, AT&T and his firm signed an agreement to form a joint venture. The point I want to make here is that such cultural misunderstandings do not break business deals, as is taught in some cross-culture seminars. There are usually deeper, more fundamental reasons in making or breaking a deal.

One such deeper, more fundamental reason that may significantly affect international business deals and cross-border management is the difference in the governance environment, such as the friction between rule-based and relation-based systems.[22]

In one of our survey studies of U.S.-Chinese joint venture operations in Shenzhen, China, we asked the Chinese employees about their relationship with the American manager. One of the interviewees, who reported to the manager directly, told us that he thought the manager did not care about him. "Why?" we asked. He said, "Well, our interaction is only about work; he never asked me personal questions, such as my family background and so on." For him, if the manager does not get personal, it means the manager does not regard him as a valuable employee. We then subtly asked the manager about what he thinks of this employee. As it turned out, the manager thought highly of the employee. We then probed him if he chatted with employees about their family and if he made an effort to know their background. "No! As you know very well, I am not supposed to nose around in their private lives!" The American manager raised his voice as if we have asked an inappropriate question.[23]

This is a typical misunderstanding between rule-based managers and relation-based employees. In a rule-based environment, the working relationship between the manager and the employee is primarily defined based on the job description, which spells out the responsibility and authorities of each post. The manager assumes the employee is capable (otherwise he would not have been hired in the first place) and expects him to perform well, unless proven otherwise. The managers should only manage the employee based on job-related information and performance and should not use age, marital status, or any other personal information or traits to reward or punish the employee.

Differences in Working Relationships Between the Two Environments

In a relation-based environment, the manager and the employee tend to spend more time to establish a good relation first. Each party will observe and test the other repeatedly to make sure that the other party is reliable and trustworthy. The manager will not fully trust a new employee unless he has been tested. Such a rationale is the opposite of the norms in rule-based working relationships. In general, the following are some differences in how workers in rule-based and relation-based environments view working relationships.[24]

1. *Scope of jobs.* Workers in rule-based and relation-based environments have different views on the scope of a job, namely, what duties, responsibilities, perquisites, and benefits are included in a job. In a rule-based environment, jobs tend to be defined narrowly in the job description, which must be in accordance with laws and regulations. In a relation-based environment, since the boss has nearly absolute power and thus has a stronger sense of "owning" the employee, the

boss may define what the employee should do at his personal preference, and he may even ask the employee to carry out personal errands. The line between work and personal life is blurred, and what is included in the job is more negotiable.

2. *Terms of working relationships.* The above leads to a second difference in working relationship between the two environments: Workers and managers in rule-based and relation-based environments differ in the *precision* of the terms of working relationships. For rule-based managers, the terms of the working relationships should follow the job description and the letter of law and regulations. But for the relation-based workers, since they weigh gaining personal favor from the manager more heavily and emphasize the establishment of a close relationship with the manager, their perception about the terms of the working relationship is beyond work-related issues and may include other activities that may enhance their personal relationship with the boss. Thus they prefer terms of the relationship to be fuzzy.

3. *Expectations of working relationships.* Correspondingly, the expectation of the working relationship is different too. Using the example of the U.S.-Chinese joint venture in Shenzhen, while the American manager views the relationship narrowly and as task oriented and purposely stays out of the employee's personal life, the Chinese employee expects that in order to build a close relationship with the manager, the manager and the employee should not only develop a good working relationship, but more importantly, they should also develop a good personal friendship that will last beyond the current work assignment. Our interview of managers who worked in relation-based countries such as Indonesia, Vietnam, and Thailand told us that they maintained friendship and correspondence with some of their coworkers and employees long after they left the job.

   Because of their expectations, relation-based employees tend to take work-related issues personally. As a study on management in Thailand showed, criticism from the expatriate manager may be interpreted by the local employee as a personal attack.[25]

4. *Investments in working relationships.* For workers and managers in a relation-based environment, since building a good relationship with coworkers, superiors, and subordinates is very important, they

are prepared and willing to invest time and resources to do so. For example, gift giving or gift exchanges are necessary parts of building relationships and tend to involve expensive gifts to show the magnitude of the effort and the commitment the gift giving signals. Invitations to each other's homes may also be used as a necessary and important occasion to build relationships.

On the other hand, to an expatriate manager from a rule-based country who holds a narrow view of the working relationships with the local employees based on job description and regulations, employees getting together at someone's home is just for fun, rather than an investment in building good working relations. Furthermore, many rule-based countries have strict laws regulating gift giving in business dealings. Thus for the expatriate manager, gift giving is at best viewed as ceremonial, which may be unnecessary. Expensive gifts are certainly frowned upon because of the implication of bribery.

5. *Differences in process priorities.* In a rule-based environment, there is a high level of generalized trust, and thus people take what they are told by strangers (new employees) more at the face value, such as a person's resume, education background, and work experience. Managers expect the workers to "hit the ground running," and the general attitude toward workers can be summed as "trustworthy unless proven otherwise." Work first, and if work goes well, coworkers, superiors, and subordinates may develop cordial working relationships. In a relation-based society, generalized trust is low. People tend to discount what they hear from someone they have just met, which implies that there may be a lower level of mutual trust between a manager and a new employee than in a rule-based environment. The manager and the employee must test each other in order to establish a level of mutual trust so that they can work together efficiently. Relationships comes first and work follows. The predominant philosophy about interpersonal trust is that anyone is presumed "untrustworthy unless proven otherwise."

Therefore, workers and managers in a relation-based environments are prepared and willing to spend more time to get to know their managers, subordinates, and coworkers, whereas managers from a rule-based country may think it is unnecessary and a waste of time. Table 5.1 summarizes the contrast in the expectations of working relationship formation between rule-based and relation-based workers and managers.

How to Improve Expatriate Performance

Based on the above analyses, we may draw the conclusion that the misunderstandings and mismatches between managers and subordinates in working relationships may be a major reason behind the high failure rate of rule-based expatriate managers working in relation-based environments. In this section we discuss different scenarios of the working relationships to help expatriate managers improve their management efficiency and effectiveness.

There are four combinations of working relationships between expatriate managers and local employees in terms of their expectations and behaviors, as shown in Figure 5.2.

Table 5.1. Expectations of Working Relationship Formation Between Rule-Based and Relation-Based Workers and Managers

Dimensions of expectations	Relation-based workers and managers	Rule-based workers and managers
Terms	Vague	Clear
Scope	Wide and deep (it may include all sorts of activities and relationship between an employer and a worker)	Narrow and specific, task oriented
Duration of the relationship	Long	Short
Views on work-related issues (criticism, discussion)	Take it personal	View it as factual, impersonal
Time needed to develop the working relationship	Long	Short
Costs of developing the relationship	High	Low
Learning curve	Flat, slow learning process, since relations are secretive and particularistic	Steep, fast learning process, since rules are by their nature transparent, public, and general

Source: Adapted from Maurer and Li (2006).

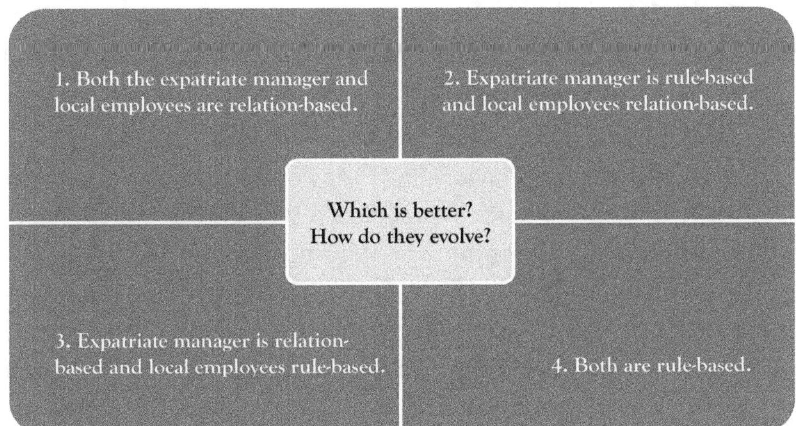

Figure 5.2. Working relationships between expatriate manager and local employees

1. *Both the expatriate manager and local employees are relation-based.* In this case, the expatriate manager completely adopts the local environment and manages the subsidiary the relation-based way. There is minimal confusion, and thus the working relationship is harmonious. Both the manager and the local employees take their time to get to know each other and build up their relationships, which implies that the time and resources used in such effort is relatively high. As we discussed earlier, when the scale and scope of a business is small, the relation-based way can be efficient. However, as the business grows larger, relying on personal relationship will become costly and inefficient. Thus, if the subsidiary has a small number of employees, using the relation-based way to manage can be efficient. Actually, it can be more efficient than the rule-based way, since the manager can manage each employee individually based on the employee's characteristics to fully realize each employee's potential. On the other hand, if the subsidiary has many employees, the relation-based way can be time consuming and even impossible. Furthermore, if the expatriate manager does not introduce any rule-based management into the organization and maintains at the status quo, he or she will hinder the growth and expansion of the subsidiary.

2. *The expatriate manager is rule-based and the local employees are relation-based.* This is the most common scenario for a multinational corporation (MNC) headquartered in a rule-based country and investing in a relation-based country. In general, it is desirable for the MNC expatriate manager to bring a new, rule-based management style to the host country that is relation-based, because, as we discussed earlier, as the scale and scope of the subsidiary grows, or more generally, as the country's economy develops, relation-based governance will become inefficient and must transform to rule-based governance. The caveat is that the expatriate manager must gauge the acceptance of rule-based management by the local employees. If the expatriate manager pushes the new management style beyond the ability to accept and lose the support of the local employees, then it will backfire and damage the working relationships. In sum, the expatriate should be fully aware of the gap between the rule-based and relation-based expectations of working relationships and should keep a healthy lead in implementing rules in the subsidiary.

3. *The expatriate manager is relation-based and the local employees are rule-based.* It is not unheard of that an MNC headquartered in a rule-based country sends an expatriate manager to a host country that is more local than the local employees. For example, an American firm operating a subsidiary in Indonesia may emphasize the conformity to the local culture and sends a manager who was born in Indonesia. However, this manager's experience with the Indonesian society may be outdated. His or her mentality may be more relation-based than that of the local employees, who may have been exposed to more rule-based practices. In this scenario, the expatriate manager fails to lead the local employees to adopt more rules in the organization. He or she must change or be replaced.

4. *Both are rule-based.* Generally speaking, this is a rare case, but an efficient one, especially if the operation is large and there are many employees. From a dynamic perspective, it is hoped that the relation-based organizations and societies will eventually migrate to the rule-based environment as they develop and expand. In this sense, it should be the objective of the expatriate manager, who was

trained and is experienced in the rule-based environment, to lead the subsidiary and its employees to evolve into a more rule-based operating environment. In order to accomplish this, the expatriate manager should first evaluate the governance environment in the assigned country, study the organizational structure and culture of the subsidiary, and formulate a management strategy that will gradually implement more rule-based management.

CHAPTER 6

Friction Between Information and Communication Technology and Relation-Based Governance

The revolution of information technology (IT) that began with the advent of the World Wide Web in the 1990s and culminated in the early 2000s has fundamentally changed the way we live and work. While many people, especially young people, take the use of IT, such as the Internet, for granted without thinking how much efficiency has been gained by using it, they may not realize that merely 2 decades ago, people would be glued to a large paper map with tiny fonts for hours to plan a trip and would desperately look for a public pay phone on the road if they were lost.

The key to understanding the IT revolution can be simplified to two basic features. The first is digitization. Information goods are content that can be digitized into a series of 1s and 0s. If the contents cannot be digitized, such as the mood of a board meeting, then it cannot be called an "information good" in the sense of IT. The second feature is the dissemination of information goods. Once the good is digitized, it can be replicated and transmitted on an extremely large scale with lightning speed virtually without boarders and limitations. The technology that enables the production and communication of information is called IT or ICT (information and communications technology); we will use these terms interchangeably in this book.

While the fact that the IT revolution has helped business to drastically improve its efficiency is widely recognized and hardly controversial, many people may not realize that the use of IT in business management and the benefit from using it differ with some interesting pattern across countries. In this chapter, we will examine how the IT revolution affects business and management practices in relation-based societies as opposed to rule-based societies.

The Use of ICT and Efficiency

To understand the cost and benefit of using ICT, we can start with looking at how a movie is made and distributed. To make a movie is not easy. First, the producer must identify a story, which is usually based on a popular novel, acquire the movie rights of the novel, convert it into a movie script, and then shoot the film, which requires a large amount of capital—tens or hundreds of millions of dollars—to hire the actors, rent studios, and so on. Once the movie has been successfully created, making an additional copy of the newly created movie is easy: If you already have a computer, you just need to buy a blank DVD+R, which costs about 25 cents or less. Based on this example, it is easy to see the cost structure of information goods: *They are costly to produce and costless to reproduce.*

From a business management perspective, if a firm wants to use ICT to fulfill its information and communication needs, it must invest resources (financial, human, and technological) to build an information technology infrastructure, which may include creating an IT department, purchasing equipment, staffing, and training all the employees to adopt and use IT. Since these expenditures are upfront and do not vary based on how many people will potentially use IT, they can be viewed as fixed costs. If there are few people in the firm who use the newly created IT system to communicate, then the average cost per user will be very high; alternatively, if there is a large number of people in the organization using the new IT infrastructure to communicate, then the average cost of using the IT system will be very low. Thus the inherent cost structure of ICT (high fixed costs and decreasing marginal cost) implies that large organizations benefit more from the use of ICT than small organizations. In a small organization, the traditional, face-to-face communication is more efficient (see Figure 6.1).[1]

Another feature of ICT that affects its adoption and use is digitization. As we briefly mentioned, only content that can be digitized can

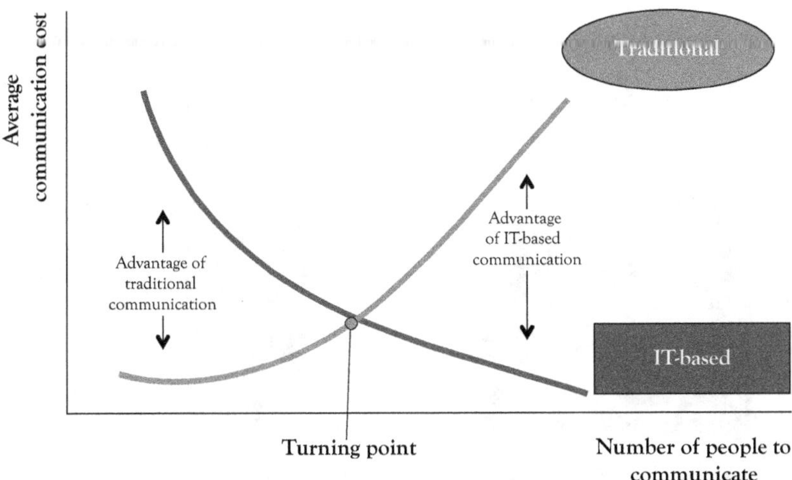

Figure 6.1. Cost of traditional versus IT-based communication

be made into information goods. In other words, in order for firms to use ICT in business operations and management, the contents must be able to be digitized. If business operations and management rely on the type of information that cannot be digitized, then ICT is not very useful. For instance, an employee comes to work to find that the mood of the office is tense, and the boss seems to be worried by something, or a business owner learns secretly that his rival played golf with a government official, then later sees his government contracts being cancelled. This kind of information is difficult to quantify and thus may not be used in decision-making models. This discussion leads to our view that *the use of ICT is more congruent with business operations and management that rely on formal decision-making processes based on quantifiable and publicly available information*

The Internet and the Relation-Based Societies

If we compare the Internet (which is like the air and water for ICT) and the governance environment of the relation-based societies, we will find some very interesting contrasts (see Figure 6.2).[2] First, the Internet is a network without a center. The network consists of millions of servers that directly or indirectly link to each other. It is a decentralized network; no

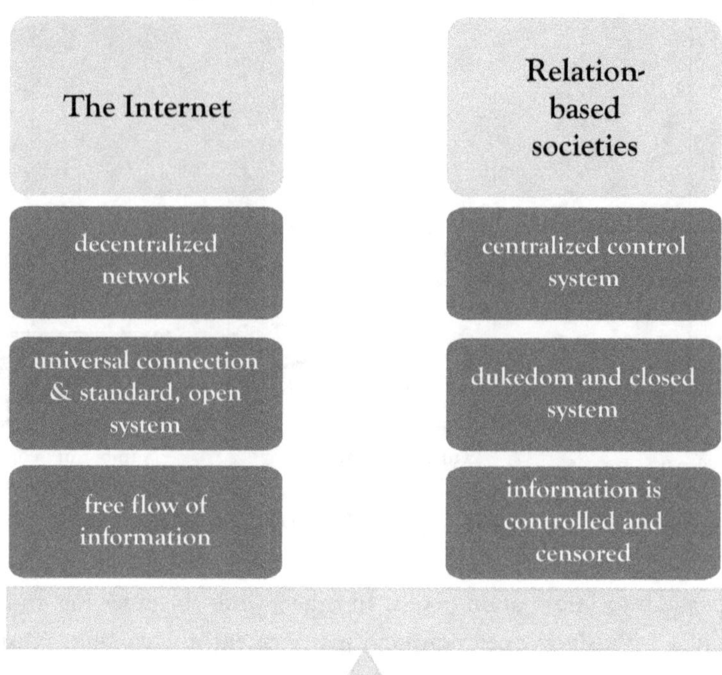

Figure 6.2. Contrasting features of the Internet- and relation-based societies

one—neither a country nor a firm or person—controls it. A relation-based society tends to be highly hierarchical, or centralized. Most are controlled by a dictator or a strong ruling circle. Second, the structure of the Internet is based on a universal platform on which different software and programs may communicate with each other through commonly recognizable protocols. A relation-based society, on the contrary, tends to maintain its own proprietary system that is not compatible with others. Third, information is free on the Internet. The very premise of the Internet is that it serves as a huge depository for all sorts of information for people to access, mostly free. In relation-based societies, much information is controlled by the state and labeled as "state secrets."

These three major differences put the Internet and the government of relation-based societies at odds, and it is not surprising that most relation-based societies try to limit the use of the Internet by citizens and firms. In a book titled *Open Networks, Closed Regimes: The Impact of the Internet on Authoritarian Rule*, the authors discussed eight governments that severely limited the use of the Internet in their countries.[3] They include China, Cuba, Singapore, Vietnam, Burma (Myanmar), United Arab Emirates, Saudi Arabia, and Egypt. As can be seen, they all are not rule-based, with perhaps Singapore being slightly more rule-based among them, whereas China and Vietnam are among the most relation-based. The fundamental question the book's authors asked is whether the Internet will help to push these closed regimes open. They concluded that the rise of the Internet poses great challenges to these authoritarian (non-rule-based) regimes, but it alone cannot end authoritarian regimes. They noted that "authoritarian regions can guide the development of the Internet so that it serves state-defined goals and priorities."[4] As for the reaction of the citizens and firms to the state control and censorship of the Internet, they observed that "Internet users may back away from politically sensitive material on the web . . . and entrepreneurs may find it more profitable to cooperate with authorities than to challenge their censorship."[5]

Yahoo!'s Dilemma in China

In 2004, the Chinese authorities asked the Hong Kong subsidiary of Yahoo!, a U.S.-based company, to submit the private e-mail records of Shi Tao, a Chinese journalist. Yahoo! obliged. The Chinese authorities used the records to sentence Shi Tao to a 10-year imprisonment for "endangering state security."[6] Yahoo!'s compliance with the Chinese authorities was heavily criticized back home in the United States. During a congressional hearing in which Yahoo! executives testified, Tom Lantos, the late U.S. congressman, blasted Yahoo!'s CEO Jerry Yang and company lawyer Michael Callahan: "Technically and financially, you are giants, but morally, you are pygmies."[7] In his congressional testimony, Yahoo! CEO Yang hinted that his company was in no position to defy such an order from the Chinese authorities.[8]

There are many similar cases in which firms or citizens are accused by a relation-based regime for using the Internet to commit a crime that "endangers state security."[9]

In addition to the clash between ICT and relation-based government at the societal level due to the three fundamental differences, the use of ICT at the firm level in relation-based societies also encounters some resistance due to the incompatibilities between ICT and the organizational culture and structure.

The Interface Between Governance and ICT in Relation-Based Organizations

Cultural Compatibility

Culture can be defined and analyzed from many different angles. We focus on a dimension that is most relevant to the rule-based versus relation-based comparison: the low-context versus high-context communications. Low-context communication refers to the style of communication that is direct, explicit, and verbal, as opposed to high-context communication, which relies on the implicitly shared references between the parties and indirect, nonverbal expressions. It is well known that the Chinese culture emphasizes high-context communication style, whereas Americans prefer a more direct style of communication.[10] In their book on Chinese communication style, Gao and Ting-Toomey cited an interesting example to illustrate the difference between American and Chinese ways of communication, which I paragraph here:

Scenario 1. Conversion between a Chinese man (C1) and another Chinese friend (C2):

C1: I am flying to New York for a vacation tomorrow! (I hope he will give me a ride to the airport.)

C2: That sounds fun! (He may need me to drive him to the airport.) Do you have someone to drive you to the airport? I can give you a ride.

Scenario 2. Conversion between an American (A1) and another American friend (A2):

A1: I am flying to New York for a vacation tomorrow! Can you give me a lift to the airport?

A2: That sounds fun! Of course, what time should I pick you up?

Scenario 3. Conversion between a Chinese (C1) and another American friend (A2):

C1: I am flying to New York for a vacation tomorrow! (I hope he will give me a ride to the airport.)

A2: That sounds fun! Have a good time! (If he needs a ride, he will ask me.)

In Scenario 1, the conversation was based on the high-context communication mode. The need to have a ride was not even mentioned; it was hinted at best. In a relation-based environment, people usually do not interact with strangers and rely on close friends to help each other. When dealing with close friends who have interacted many times and known each other well, direct, explicit communication is not necessary; relying on implicit messages and hints are sufficient. Furthermore, the indirectness in asking a favor may save face if the other party cannot fulfill the favor, preserving the good relationship.

On the contrary, Scenario 2 is based on a rule-based environment in which business and social exchanges tend to be conducted at "arm's length" between people who meet for the first time. Dealing with strangers is part of one's daily life and work. In such a situation, direct and explicit communication is the only way to effectively convey what you mean rather than subtle hints for which shared experience and mutual references are a prerequisite to comprehend.

Obviously, a misunderstanding occurs in Scenario 3, when the rule-based way meets the relation-based way.

As we discussed earlier, the contents of ICT must be the information that can be digitized. Many types of high-context information, such as hints, shared past experiences, or the mood of the message, cannot be digitized and thus cannot be stored and transmitted through ICT, limiting the use of ICT in a relation-based organization. Next we discuss some specific issues that relation-based firms face in adopting ICT in their management and operations.

Informational Compatibility

A management information system (MIS) is an ICT-based internal control tool that integrates and analyzes business operation and management-related information to aid strategy formulation and decision making in an organization. For MIS to function, it must rely on and can only process digitized and codified information. However, a great deal of information within an organization that is vital for strategy formulation and decision making, such as the mood in the factory, gossip, rumors, or the conflict between two managers, cannot be digitized, as Mintzberg noted.[11]

An encounter between a researcher with a local business leader in Vietnam may illustrate informal and yet efficient information gathering:

> "I know where you were this morning," the leader of one of the largest land development companies in HCMC [Ho Chi Minh City] told me. I was startled by this revelation, since I had not told him I had been interviewing another company that morning. I was not aware of any connection between the two companies because I had been introduced to them through different people.[12]

Later, the researcher learned that leader had an informal network that extended to the other company she interviewed.

The rumor that a firm's major client was seen having a long conversation with a competitor of the firm at an industry gathering cannot be verified or quantified for entry into the MIS database to be analyzed. But several months later the MIS database showed that a contract with the client was not renewed. In a relation-based environment, this type of information is more important than that in a rule-based environment for business intelligence and decision making, as most deals are based on private relationships. So, due to the lack of informational compatibility, the use of MIS in relation-based firms is more limited.

Decision Mode Compatibility

The decision mode of relation-based firms does not have a high compatibility with MIS aided by ICT for the following reasons.

First, MIS is most efficient in disseminating large amounts of information to many users. With the aid of ICT and MIS, an entry-level manager may have access to as much information about the market competition and firm's operation as the firm's CEO (of course, excluding confidential information as such board meetings or other information on a need-to-know basis). This democratization of information access has greatly empowered the rank-and-file staff members and managers to make decisions on their own and has consequently made the modern organizations more flat and flexible in terms of decision making. Of course, the above scenario is only possible if the vital information, such as market intelligence and intraorganizational information, can be digitized, which tends to be more the case in rule-based rather than relation-based firms.

Second, for relation-based firms, most vital information for decision making is secretive (as private relationships tend to be secretive and exclusive) and controlled by the head of the firm. The reasons for this are that first, private relationships are hard to delegate, so the big boss must tend them in person; second, due to the lack of exit options for the subordinates in a relation-based firm (see chapter 5), they are unlikely to voice their honest opinions and take responsibilities to make decisions, which in turn makes centralizing decision making a necessity, and the boss usually relies on his gut feeling about the market (which lacks publicly verifiable information) and his private relationships with other key players in the market, nullifying the use of MIS for decision making.

Mode of Vertical Communications

In our survey on IT governance and usage in American and Chinese firms, we found an interesting difference between American and Chinese managers and professional staffs. We asked both American and Chinese respondents to what degree they use ICT to communicate (a) with their supervisors and (b) with their subordinates. We found that Americans reported that they use ICT to communicate with their subordinates and bosses more or less equally (with the use of ICT for upward communication being slightly higher), and the Chinese managers indicated that they use more ICT to communicate with their subordinates than with their bosses. What can we make out of this difference?

As we just discussed, people in a rule-based environment tend to use low-context information, which can be more easily digitized and transmitted by ICT. Furthermore, in a rule-based environment, rules tend to be equally applied to everybody, including both the supervisor and subordinates, so there should not be a systematic difference in using ICT for upward or downward communications. In a relation-based environment, in addition to the fact that high-context communication is often used, which is difficult to be conveyed via ICT, the relationship between a supervisor and a subordinate is more unequal than in a rule-based environment. In other words, using culture scholar Hofstede's term,[13] there is a greater *power distance* in relation-based organizations. Digitized information, such as e-mail, is viewed as cold, faceless, and certainly not something that can be used to cultivate cordial, personal relationships. In a relation-based setting, the subordinates tend to have a strong motivation to cultivate a warm, individual relationship with the boss. And understandably, the motivation to develop a good relationship with a boss is expectedly stronger than in rule-based environments. Thus our survey results may reflect the fact that while bosses may use ICT to reach down, most people prefer the more personalized mode, such as face-to-face, when communicating with their superiors in relation-based countries like China.

The Commitment Problem

Adopting IT in operation and management may jeopardize existing relationships, including relationships within a firm between manager and staff and relationships between firms. The reason for this is that IT, especially the Internet, drastically reduces the search cost for market information and new partners, making long-term commitment to relationships, such as a supplier relationships or any employment relationship, harder to maintain. For example, a story told by Guo Fansheng, the CEO of Huicong Company in China, vividly illustrates the conflict between the introduction of IT and the reliance on relations. As all executives know, a major headache in most purchase departments is that the purchasing manager may take kickbacks, which are difficult to verify and punish. So when Guo selected a purchasing manager, he would put paramount importance on the loyalty and integrity of the candidate and test and retest to make sure he or she was trustworthy so that he could make a long-term commitment to this relationship. Such a relation-based arrangement worked fine until the Internet arrived. Once his firm needed to make a major purchase, he ordered his purchasing manager to get bids and the manager presented the best bid to Guo. Out of curiosity, Guo put an anonymous message on a purchasing Web site to solicit bids. Many bids came in and, not surprisingly, some of them were lower than the best bid his manager presented to him. The difference was as wide as over 1 million yuan ($140,000). Guo was furious. He called the manager in, showed him the lower bids he got from the Web, and asked him if he had taken any kickback. The manager adamantly rejected his accusation. Guo said, "Then you must be grossly incompetent, and either way, you're fired."[14]

Did Guo do the right thing to fire the manager? He hinted that it may not be a well-thought-out decision, since it is very likely that with an opening bid on the net, it is almost certain that he will find a lower bid than his manager can get through his own established personal network. The conclusion Guo drew was to open the purchasing process to the Internet. Of course, in doing so, he may have lost some capable purchasing staff members who may feel that their expertise—cultivating long-term relationships with suppliers—is threatened.

How ICT Affects Corporate Governance

From our analysis above, while firms in the rule-based environment have substantially improved their efficiency through the use of ICT and MIS in operation management and strategic decision making, it is clear that due to its culture, information and communication mode, and decision mode, *the use of ICT and MIS in relation-based firms is more limited to processes that can be easily digitized*, such as processing paychecks, automating production, and bookkeeping (the use of MIS in accounting may be limited as relation-based firms manipulate accounting information more heavily, as we showed in chapter 3). The conventional wisdom predicts that with the adoption of ICT, which puts all firms in an equal footing, firms in developing countries will leapfrog to catch up to the firms in the developed world in productivity and efficiency. Based on our analysis, this may not be the case if the firms in developing countries are relation-based and limit their use of ICT only to simple processes. Their gains in efficiency from the use of ICT may not be as big as that of their counterparts in rule-based environments. Thus it is possible that the gap in ICT-based efficiency gain may be widening instead of narrowing. On the other hand, in the increasingly globalized market, *the competitive pressure from the rule-based firms that have made substantial gains from fuller adoption of ICT will force relation-based firms to transform themselves into more rule-based firms so that they can become more competitive as they grow and expand beyond their traditional domain.* And, indeed, a greater effort to realize the potential from the adoption of ICT in true decision making will help them in the process.

CHAPTER 7

"Efficiency Enhancing" Corruption?

Corruption in Relation-Based Societies

Corruption in international business is a major challenge for both multinational corporations and governments, including the multinationals' home-country government and the government of the countries these companies invest in. After reading the previous chapters on the characteristics of the relation-based markets, the reader may have the impression that corruption may be more prevalent in relation-based societies, which, as will be shown later in this chapter, is correct. In this chapter, we will discuss how corruption is carried out in societies with different governance environments and how it affects the economy.

Corruption Is Bad for Society as a Whole, as Well as for Corrupt Officials

Corruption by government officials, which refers to the sales of government goods or services for the corrupt official's private gains, is epidemic worldwide. It ranges from multi-billion-dollar government projects illegally awarded to private businesspeople who bribe the officials in charge, to petty corruption in which a policeman extorts cash from a hapless tourist who does not know what laws he has broken.

Scholars of political economy have long argued that corruption is bad for a society because the citizens and firms are the ones that have to pay for the corruption, and those payments will be displaced from productive use by the citizens and firms. Furthermore, corrupt officials, for fear of being caught, usually hide the ill-gotten wealth in secret places, which is not always the optimal way to employ capital. A third reason that corruption is bad for the economy is that it distorts the allocation of resources in a society. The corrupt officials have a strong incentive to use their power to encourage the type of businesses that are easy for them to extort, such as complicated projects that require many approvals, so that at each approval the official in charge can ask for bribes. An example of these projects is real estate development in many countries. Another kind of resource-distortion project is the expensive, one of a kind, custom-designed project that cannot be easily benchmarked so that the corrupt official and the briber can collude to jack up the total cost and split the illegal gains. Projects of this sort include nuclear power plants and mega construction projects such as airports and highways. Corruption-induced distortion has plagued many underdeveloped countries. For instance, when traveling in poverty-ridden African countries, one would see underfunded and rundown elementary schools but expensive highways that could be used for landing airplanes. A possible reason for this disparity is that the cost of building new schools can be relatively easy to calculate on a per-student basis and thus has little room for squeezing out a bribe to pay officials, whereas the construction of an expensive highway is a more lucrative project for seeping funds.

In conclusion, corruption can be said to be universally bad. It is even bad for the corrupt officials—because they face the prospect of being locked up in prison or even executed in certain countries such as China. It is a vicious cycle: More corruption makes an economy poorer; a poorer economy makes the per capita income lower and thus the corrupt official's paycheck smaller, which prompts the corrupt official to extort more bribes, increasing his chance of being caught.[1] Logically, we can argue that cleaning up corruption is beneficial for the *corrupt* officials because as the society has more resources freed from corruption to invest in the economy, the per capita income will rise and so will the official's income. The higher income of the officials reduces the drive for extorting bribes, which reduces their chance of being caught. The success stories of Hong Kong and Singapore in fighting corruption are cases in point.[2]

How Bad Is Corruption Worldwide?

In order to assess how bad corruption is in different countries, we need some quantitative data. It is difficult to get reliable corruption data, since neither the corrupt official nor the businessman who pays bribes to officials is willing to tell a surveyor about their illegal activities. Most corruption data are indirect estimates. The most used measurement of corruption across countries is the Corruption Perception Index (CPI) developed by Transparency International (TI), an international nongovernmental organization headquartered in Berlin.[3] TI conducts an annual survey of business executives, financial journalists, and country experts about their perception of corruption for each country and builds its CPI database accordingly. The CPI ranges from zero (totally corrupt) to 10 (free of corruption). Table 7.1 shows TI's estimates of the 2008 CPI in the world.

If we use a CPI score of 5.0 as a rough middle point to divide the less corrupt and more corrupt countries, we have 47 countries that are less corrupt (with scores from 5.1 to 9.3) and 133 countries that are more corrupt (with scores ranging from 1.0 to 5.0). This spread reveals that countries that suffer from corruption greatly outnumber those countries that are less corrupt.

Corruption and the Governance Environment

A closer look at the data would indicate that the more corrupt countries tend to be less rule-based. If we overlay the GEI and the corruption score (see Figure 7.1), we can see that *the more rule-based a country is, the cleaner (less corrupt) it tends to be.*

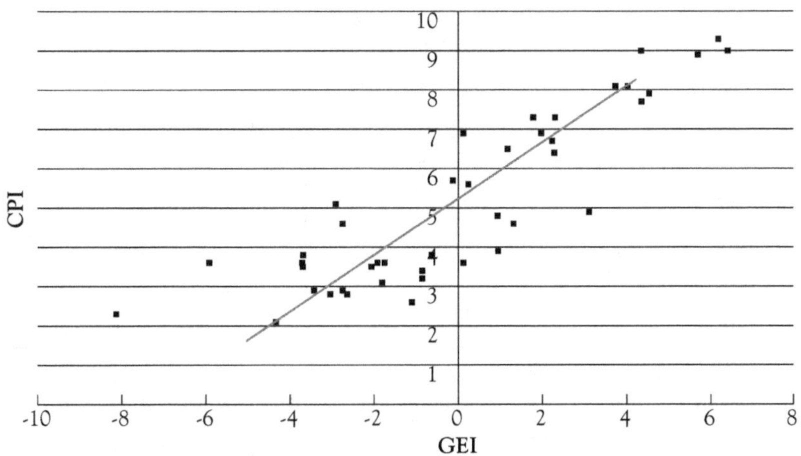

Figure 7.1. Governance environment index and corruption perception index

Note: X = GEI (high = rule-based); Y = CPI (low = corrupt).

Sources: Chapter 2 of this book and Transparency International (2008).

Table 7.1. 2008 Corruption Perception Index

Rank	Country	CPI	Rank	Country	CPI	Rank	Country	CPI
1	Denmark	9.3	61	Namibia	4.5	121	Nepal	2.7
1	New Zealand	9.3	62	Croatia	4.4	121	Nigeria	2.7
1	Sweden	9.3	62	Samoa	4.4	121	São Tomé and Príncipe	2.7
4	Singapore	9.2	62	Tunisia	4.4	121	Togo	2.7
5	Finland	9.0	65	Cuba	4.3	121	Vietnam	2.7
5	Switzerland	9.0	65	Kuwait	4.3	126	Eritrea	2.6
7	Iceland	8.9	67	El Salvador	3.9	126	Ethiopia	2.6
7	Netherlands	8.9	67	Georgia	3.9	126	Guyana	2.6
9	Australia	8.7	67	Ghana	3.9	126	Honduras	2.6
9	Canada	8.7	70	Colombia	3.8	126	Indonesia	2.6
11	Luxembourg	8.3	70	Romania	3.8	126	Libya	2.6
12	Austria	8.1	72	Bulgaria	3.6	126	Mozambique	2.6
12	Hong Kong	8.1	72	China	3.6	126	Uganda	2.6
14	Germany	7.9	72	Macedonia (former Yugoslav Republic of)	3.6	134	Comoros	2.5
14	Norway	7.9	72	Mexico	3.6	134	Nicaragua	2.5
16	Ireland	7.7	72	Peru	3.6	134	Pakistan	2.5
16	United Kingdom	7.7	72	Suriname	3.6	134	Ukraine	2.5
18	Belgium	7.3	72	Swaziland	3.6	138	Liberia	2.4
18	Japan	7.3	72	Trinidad and Tobago	3.6	138	Paraguay	2.4
18	United States	7.3	80	Brazil	3.5	138	Tonga	2.4
21	Saint Lucia	7.1	80	Burkina Faso	3.5	141	Cameroon	2.3
22	Barbados	7.0	80	Morocco	3.5	141	Iran	2.3
23	Chile	6.9	80	Saudi Arabia	3.5	141	Philippines	2.3
23	France	6.9	80	Thailand	3.5	141	Yemen	2.3
23	Uruguay	6.9	85	Albania	3.4	145	Kazakhstan	2.2
26	Slovenia	6.7	85	India	3.4	145	Timor-Leste	2.2
27	Estonia	6.6	85	Madagascar	3.4	147	Bangladesh	2.1
28	Qatar	6.5	85	Montenegro	3.4	147	Kenya	2.1
28	Saint Vincent and the Grenadines	6.5	85	Panama	3.4	147	Russia	2.1
28	Spain	6.5	85	Senegal	3.4	147	Syria	2.1
31	Cyprus	6.4	85	Serbia	3.4	151	Belarus	2.0

Rank	Country	CPI	Rank	Country	CPI	Rank	Country	CPI
32	Portugal	6.1	92	Algeria	3.2	151	Central African Republic	2.0
33	Dominica	6.0	92	Bosnia and Herzegovina	3.2	151	Côte d'Ivoire	2.0
33	Israel	6.0	92	Lesotho	3.2	151	Ecuador	2.0
35	United Arab Emirates	5.9	92	Sri Lanka	3.2	151	Laos	2.0
36	Botswana	5.8	96	Benin	3.1	151	Papua New Guinea	2.0
36	Malta	5.8	96	Gabon	3.1	151	Tajikistan	2.0
36	Puerto Rico	5.8	96	Guatemala	3.1	158	Angola	1.9
39	Taiwan	5.7	96	Jamaica	3.1	158	Azerbaijan	1.9
40	South Korea	5.6	96	Kiribati	3.1	158	Burundi	1.9
41	Mauritius	5.5	96	Mali	3.1	158	Congo, Republic	1.9
41	Oman	5.5	102	Bolivia	3.0	158	Gambia	1.9
43	Bahrain	5.4	102	Djibouti	3.0	158	Guinea-Bissau	1.9
43	Macao	5.4	102	Dominican Republic	3.0	158	Sierra Leone	1.9
45	Bhutan	5.2	102	Lebanon	3.0	158	Venezuela	1.9
45	Czech Republic	5.2	102	Mongolia	3.0	166	Cambodia	1.8
47	Cape Verde	5.1	102	Rwanda	3.0	166	Kyrgyzstan	1.8
47	Costa Rica	5.1	102	Tanzania	3.0	166	Turkmenistan	1.8
47	Hungary	5.1	109	Argentina	2.9	166	Uzbekistan	1.8
47	Jordan	5.1	109	Armenia	2.9	166	Zimbabwe	1.8
47	Malaysia	5.1	109	Belize	2.9	171	Congo, Democratic Republic	1.7
52	Latvia	5.0	109	Moldova	2.9	171	Equatorial Guinea	1.7
52	Slovakia	5.0	109	Solomon Islands	2.9	173	Chad	1.6
54	South Africa	4.9	109	Vanuatu	2.9	173	Guinea	1.6
55	Italy	4.8	115	Egypt	2.8	173	Sudan	1.6
55	Seychelles	4.8	115	Malawi	2.8	176	Afghanistan	1.5
57	Greece	4.7	115	Maldives	2.8	177	Haiti	1.4
58	Lithuania	4.6	115	Mauritania	2.8	178	Iraq	1.3
58	Poland	4.6	115	Niger	2.8	178	Myanmar	1.3
58	Turkey	4.6	115	Zambia	2.8	180	Somalia	1.0

Source: Transparency International (2008).

The average corruption score for the more rule-based countries (i.e., GEI is positive) is 6.9, whereas the corruption score for the less rule-based countries (GEI is negative) is 3.4. The non-rule-based countries, namely, the relation-based countries and the family-based countries, tend to have higher levels of corruption.

Corruption and Economic Efficiency

A further examination would show that most of the less corrupt countries are affluent while the more corrupt countries are poor. Thus the political economists are right that corruption is bad for a country's economy, as shown by Figure 7.2: The higher the corruption level, the lower the income level in a country.

So far we have only examined the relationship between corruption and income level. However, if we plot annual economic growth rate against corruption level, the trend is much less clear. In terms of economic *growth*, there are some corrupt countries that have had quite impressive economic growth, despite high corruption, such as China. Upon further examination, we can see that while economic growth rates of the less corrupt countries (mostly rich) fall in a narrower band, the economic growth rates of the more corrupt countries spread widely, from negative to highly positive (see Figure 7.3). In other words, it seems that while many corrupt countries suffered slow or negative economic growth, some enjoyed very rapid economic growth. How do we explain this?

Why Do Some Economies Grow Fast Despite Corruption?

Political economists have long conjectured that corruption may help economic efficiencies in some ways.[4] For example, in a communist economy, the government exerts absolute control over virtually all production and consumption activities and thus takes away any incentives for the bureaucrats to take any efficiency-enhancing initiatives or engage in any productive activities. Under such a circumstance, business activities are extremely slow and getting permission to do business is difficult. To incentivize the

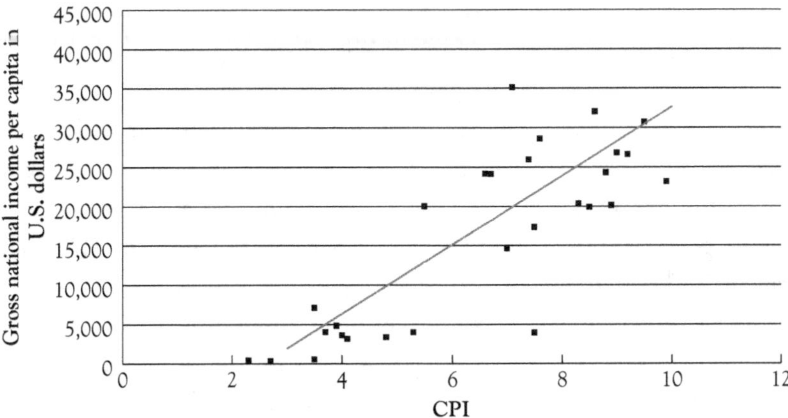

Figure 7.2. Corruption level and income level across countries

Note: Y = gross national income per capita in U.S. dollars; X = Corruption Perception Index; 0 = most corrupt, and 10 = most clean.

Source: Transparency International (2008) and World Bank (2000).

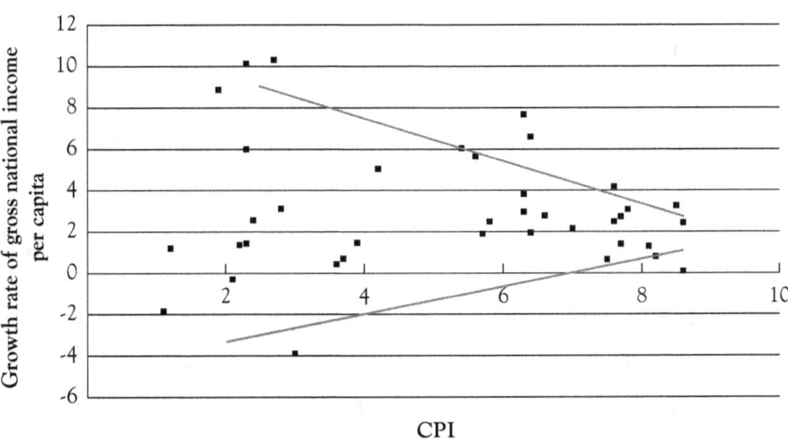

Figure 7.3. Corruption level and economic growth

Note: Y = growth rate of gross national income per capita in U.S. dollars; X = Corruption Perception Index; 0 = most corrupt, and 10 = most clean.

Source: Transparency International (2008); World Bank (2000).

bureaucrats to loosen up their control and make doing business possible, bribery may be necessary. Actually, this is what happens in most reforming economies in which the government is powerful and monopolizes most of the country's resources. Bribing the officials who can make business possible is what one might call "greasing the wheels." Thus some political economists argue that some corruption is necessary to liberalize a rigid government-controlled economy. Scholars use the term "efficiency enhancing" to describe such corruption.[5]

What social conditions will make corruption less predatory (or more efficiency enhancing)? Our study shows that in relation-based societies, corruption tends to be more efficiency enhancing.[6] The main reason is that compared to other non-rule-based societies such as the family-based ones, the relation-based societies tend to have a higher level of trust.

The Role of Trust in Corruption

It sounds paradoxical that corruption, an illegal activity in most societies, would need trust, which is associated with honesty and integrity, to be carried out. This is precisely because it is illegal, so trust between the briber and the corrupt official is crucial. When a corrupt official is contemplating taking a bribe, he must evaluate his risk—the risk of being caught and the subsequent punishment he may receive if being caught. Furthermore, there is also a risk of being cheated in a bribery-corruption transaction. While small-time corruption can be simultaneously transacted, such as a policeman extorting payment from a driver who was stopped for a traffic violation, large-scale corruption involving huge amounts of bribes and multiyear projects usually cannot be completed on a spot. The bribe payment and the delivery of the promised goods, such as a license, approval, or government projects, tend to be separated in time and space. In such cases, there is always the age-old question in trade: Who should do it first? Should the corrupt official deliver the desired government goods or service first, or should the briber pay first?

If the corrupt official and the briber trust each other highly, then the temporal and spatial separation of payment and delivery is not a problem. Otherwise, when there is little trust between the two parties, a bribery-corruption transaction will be difficult because each party is afraid of being cheated by the other. This fear is further exacerbated by the fact that neither party can resort to the legal system for protection, since paying and taking bribes is illegal in all countries. For the corrupt official, there is an added risk of being blackmailed by the briber.

Once again, this is why trust plays an important role in corruption, which sounds paradoxical because in most cultures trust is associated with integrity and honesty, whereas corruption means conspiring in secrecy and is criminal. But following our analysis, readers will see that the relationship between trust and corruption is not black and white.

As we discussed in chapter 2, trust is the confidence or faith one places on another person or other people. What are the implications of having or not having a high level of trust in a bribery-corruption relationship? We can use logical deduction to help us better understand this issue.

Suppose there are two societies: A and B. In Society A, there is a high level of trust (note that we don't have to distinguish generalized or particularized trust), whereas in Society B, trust is almost nonexistent. In Society A, corrupt officials feel safe to take bribes from almost anyone, as the chance of being turned in by the briber is extremely low, due to the high level of trust. Bribers are confident to pay in advance and, likewise, corrupt officials can deliver the requested government goods and services first. The separation of payment and delivery in time and space does not pose a problem. Thus the corrupt official can sell his service (such as a government contract) to the highest bidding briber, who does not have to be a relative or close friend of the corrupt official but must be a highly efficient businessperson, which enables him to pay a high bribe and can still make a profit (provided that all the bidders more or less maintain similar qualities for their products or services). Under such an environment, bribery-corruption becomes a competitive market and the most efficient briber gets the economic opportunities controlled by the government, making corruption "efficiency enhancing."

In Society B, there is little trust among people. Corrupt officials do not dare to take bribes from people they don't know well. In other words, they must keep such illegal deals within a very small circle of confidants—their family members and very few close friends. However, their cronies may not be in the right industry to take advantage of the opportunities the officials can provide, and the cronies' firms may be inefficient with low productivity. Thus, in general, corruption does not lead to efficiency enhancing in such societies.

Furthermore, in Society B, if the government controls vast resources and the politicians are powerful, they must use their power and resources to extort rent (payment) from the society (citizens and businesses). Since the officials are afraid of engaging in bribery-delivery relationships as illustrated in the case of Society A, then they will extort payment from the society by force, such as announcing new taxes or imposing fees on businesses. What is worse is that the corrupt official does not have to deliver any government goods or services in such top-down extortions. As a result, corruption becomes *predatory*. It is an absolute loss for the society.

The next question is, among the societies with high levels of corruption (mostly not rule-based), which ones tend to have a higher level of trust? Chapter 2 has answered this question: The relation-based societies have a higher level of extended particularized trust than the family-based societies. These societies are more like Society A in our example, and corruption in these societies tends to be more "efficiency enhancing," whereas the family-based societies closely approximate Society B, with little trust beyond the family, and corruption in those societies is more "predatory." In the next section, we use cases of corruption in China and the Philippines to illustrate these two types of corruption.[7]

Corruption in China and the Philippines

China and the Philippines are developing countries with similar income levels, and both have experienced high levels of corruption. But the similarity seems to end there; what differs between the two is that China has a much higher level of trust and a higher level of economic growth rate, as can be seen from Table 7.2.

Table 7.2. Corruption, Trust, and Economic Development in China and the Philippines

Country	GDP annual growth rate (%) (1990–2000)	GNI per capita (2001)	CPI (10 = best; 1 = worst; 2000)	Trust (1999–2004)
Philippines	3.3	1050	2.8	8.6
China	10.3	890	3.1	54.5

Sources: Transparency International (2008); World Bank (2000); World Value Survey (2005).

Corruption in China

As we know, China is a typical relation-based society, in which *guanxi-based* networks have been extensively developed and widely spread. These informal social networks were first established during the era of Mao Zedong's rule (1949–1976) and were booming and dominant in China during the later years of Mao's ruling, during which the economy was on the verge of total collapse and consumer goods were in extreme shortage. In order to obtain daily necessities, jobs, or permission to move from one place to another, people resorted to a gray market for consumer goods and government goods and services that were distributed through these informal social networks based on exchanges of favors. After Mao died in 1976, the Chinese government led by Deng called for a market economy and encouraged people to make money. At the same time when the economy took off at a rapid pace, the formal legal system was underdeveloped: Laws were and still are made by one party—the Chinese Communist Party—in which judges are political appointees and corruption is rampant. As a result, people and firms in China rely on relation-based governance to protect their business interests.

Those informal social networks are based on extended particularized trust. A common practice in China is informal networking. For instance, in social gatherings or parties, a businessperson may mention that he is trying to get a project approved by a particular government department, but he does not know anyone there and will ask around if someone at the gathering knows officials in that department. Then someone in the party may volunteer (and will get compensated if he does help), "I don't know anyone there directly, but my sister-in-law's father has a former student who works there," and then this person would introduce this official to the businessman who was looking for help. Once the official and the businessman are introduced, they can quickly begin to negotiate a deal, which usually involves the businessman paying the official and the latter delivering the needed service to the former.

In a society that lacks trust, such a deal may be viewed as too risky. But in China, a deal in which an official is paid for a special service is quite common and the risk is quite low because although the two do not know each other well, they are introduced by people who know both of them well (a third party—see chapter 2) and can hold them accountable should they cheat. In other words, the strong particularized trust within each circle and the easy connection of one circle with another make such a bribery-corruption relationship easy to establish and operate.

In *Losing the New China*, an insightful book about corruption in China, Ethan Gutmann vividly documents how multinational companies use bribes to get around China's corrupt market. These multinational corporations would set aside big "slush funds" and hire consultants to run these funds. The consultant would use the fund secretly to bribe government officials according to the agenda set by the corporations. A multinational firm's senior executive described one such operation this way: "The terms of the deal was [*sic*] . . . a ten million dollar discretionary fund. Hands off, no questions asked. Don't ask [the consultant] where the money goes . . . We know exactly what he was up to, and exactly how successful he would be."[8]

In China, such business-to-official transactions are so frequent that there is a need to provide discrete, secure places for them to make such deals. Some smart restaurant owners saw this opportunity and offered just the right environment for them. In Beijing, an expensive Cantonese seafood restaurant with several locations was known for such a service. The following is a description by a reliable source who wishes to remain anonymous:

> I [the briber] invite my client [corrupt official] to a well-known Cantonese restaurant with several branches in Beijing. The meal costs an astronomical 20,000 rmb [$2,400] for two. On the way out, the restaurant passes a gift to my client and the client is told he or she can exchange the gift for cash if he or she does not like it. The gift is then exchanged by my client for about 10,000 rmb. I have not discussed any such exchanges with my client. But just in case people get the wrong impression, the restaurant has covered my car's license plate in the restaurant's parking lot.

As one can imagine, this kind of bribery-corruption deal is only possible when the trust between the parties is high.

Even the Chinese government realizes that corruption has reached a point that is difficult to control. A study that followed 47 corruption cases in 2007 and calculated that on average, these corrupt officials took 35 million yuan ($4 million) in bribes. The Chinese Supreme Court and the Supreme Prosecutorial Commission explicitly promulgated 10 corruption activities that are illegal. Of the 10 types of bribery-corruption behavior, the one that is most relevant to our discussion here is "an official gives a favor to someone and receives payment after the official leaves his post." Another feature of Chinese corruption is globalization: The corrupt official delivers the favor inside China and receives payment overseas in the form of luxury homes, Swiss bank accounts, gambling trips, or scholarships for the official's children to attend schools abroad. Clearly, the separation of time and space in the transaction needs a high level of trust to make such bribery-corruption deals possible.

Corruption in the Philippines

As can be seen from Table 7.2, the trust level in the Philippines is extremely low, which is an indication of a family-based environment (see chapter 2). Unlike corruption in China, corruption in the Philippines has been characterized by a pattern in which the state head would control the entry of an industry or simply monopolize it, impose a tax or surcharge on all the firms in or products of the industry, or extract a fee on firms for entering the industry. After that, the state head would then appoint one of his cronies to be in charge of the industry and steal all the collections from the state coffers. To the private sector payers, these taxes, surcharges, or fees were nothing more than robbery, a deadweight loss in the economic sense. The collecting officials simply imposed the fees on the payers without facilitating or helping any business activities. Furthermore, the victim of the corruption, the payers, would have no evidence to implicate corrupt officials (the collector of these charges) because the latter was simply carrying out a state order.

Several cases of major industries in the Philippines demonstrate this kind of corruption pattern.[9] In the coconut sector during the 1970s (accounting for roughly 25% of the Philippines' export income), former President Ferdinand Marcos imposed a tax on all sales of coconuts and copra. The agency in charge of collecting this tax was headed by his close friend Manuel Conjuangco. Conjuangco used the extorted money to buy banks, which in turn funded his acquisition of many coconut oil pressing mills. Then he put all the tax money into a fund and used the fund to subsidize the mills he and Marcos controlled.

A similar corruption pattern occurred in the cigarette industry as well. In 1975, Marcos imposed a 100% import duty on cigarette filters but gave a special 90% import duty reduction to the Philippine Tobacco Filters Corporation, a company owned by one of his cronies, Herminio Disini. Disini in turn supplied the filter at below-market prices to Fortune Tobacco, a major cigarette maker owned by another Marcos ally, Lucio Tan. Together they drove the competition out of market and monopolized the cigarette industry.

The corruption in the sugar industry resembled a similar pattern. In 1974, Marcos ordered that all sugar exports be monopolized by the Philippine Exchange Company, which was controlled by his schoolmate Robert Benidicto. With the privilege given by Marcos, Benidicto manipulated sugar prices to profit at the expense of sugar farmers and producers in the country.

In all these corruption cases, there was little cooperation between the briber (the payer of the surcharges, entry fees, and other types of extortions) and the corrupt official. The bribers were forced to pay, and the official did not enhance the efficiency of their business. It is estimated that through these extortions, Marcos and his associates amassed wealth valued at between $3 billion to $6 billion!

More Countries Follow the Same Pattern

To further verify our argument, we also conducted a statistical test using pooled data in two time periods (1994–1999 and 2000–2005) from 53 countries. We examined how corruption level and trust level affect economic growth rate in a country while controlling other important factors that may also affect economic growth. These controlled factors include income per capita, schooling, the political system, and time period. We paid special attention to the interaction of corruption level and trust level in a country.

The results support our view: The negative effect of corruption on economic growth is mitigated by a higher level of trust in a country. For example, if in a country the trust level is 0 (which means that 0% of people trust others), then the effect of corruption on economic growth would be –0.17%; however, as the level of trust increases, it will mitigate the negative effect of corruption on economic growth. On average, every 10% increase in trust would reduce the negative effect of corruption on economic growth rate by 0.03%.[10]

What can readers take away from this chapter? First, we are not saying that corruption is good. As we mentioned at the opening of the chapter, corruption has a negative effect on economic growth in all countries. However, this negative effect may be reduced when corruption interacts with a high level of extended particularized trust. Second, since the briber and the corrupt official both benefit from the deal, the briber has little incentive to turn in the corrupt official, making corruption difficult to detect. In general, we conclude that *the high level of extended particularized trust in societies with predominantly "efficiency-enhancing" corruption implies that cleaning up corruption is very difficult.* A strong and thick social network makes it very hard for "whistle blowing." Our analysis suggests that the prospect for eradicating corruption in highly relation-based countries, such as China, is not good.

CHAPTER 8

The Greatest Leap Forward

The Transition From Relation-Based to Rule-Based Governance

CITIC's (Failed) Attempt to Change the Old Way of Doing Business

In the late 1990s, in order to modernize its business operation, China International Trust and Investment Corp (CITIC; then the largest state-owned investment company) asked the consulting powerhouse McKinsey to develop an information system for its risk management. The system used statistical models that, based on the information about loan applicants, predicted the risks of issuing loans to them. After months of intense model building and testing, and some $1 million in consulting fees, McKinsey delivered the system to CITIC for use. Facing the issue of the high rate of bad loans and with great expectations of the model, the headquarters of CITIC issued a memo to all its branch offices that from now on, they should use the model to screen their loan applicants. When staff at local branches used the model, they found something very odd: Some firms that were known to be high risk received very high credit scores from the model, and the firms that had been good clients for a long time failed the model test.

These paradoxical results from the use of the model made the local branches loan officers confused. But they quickly realized why: Risk management models must rely on accurate information about the loan takers. Such a system requires a business environment in which publicly available financial information about firms is trustworthy—where firms follow the laws to accurately report their operation data. But in a relation-based society like China, public information about business credit was nonexistent, and self-reported financial information was extremely unreliable. It was well known that accounting firms would help companies to "window-dress" in order to get financing. Furthermore, the loan takers who maintained a good history of payment might not necessarily run a financially sound business; they might simply have good relations with the government so that they would get subsidized by the government when their own cash flow was short. Those subtle relation-based "assets" might not be shown in the rule-based risk model.

Thus, after hearing the complaints from the local branches and realizing that it was not practical to use the McKinsey model in China's current business environment, the headquarters issued another memo saying that the McKinsey model is for *future* use, and now the branches should go back to the traditional way of evaluating applicants and managing loans.[1]

The Greatest Leap Forward

The CITIC example highlights the difficulty of transforming from relation-based business practices to a more rule-based way, which is the theme of this concluding chapter. As a relation-based economy expands, the relation-based way of conducting and governing the business will lose its cost advantage and must adopt the rule-based way of doing business. If we look at all the economic reforms that are currently being carried out in many economies around the world, we will find that a common theme among all of them is to reduce the old relation-based way and institute more public rules that are more fair, transparent, and universally applied. In this sense, the economic reforms and transitions that have swept across nearly half of the world (mostly former communist and authoritarian-ruled countries) in the past 3 decades or so and are still going strong can be viewed as the greatest leap forward from relations to rules.[2]

The evidence of the transition is ample in many of the former and current relation-based societies. The 1997 financial crisis forced South Korea, which had been undergoing the transition for years, to go further toward a more rule-based governance system.[3] In Thailand, as the economy expanded globally, businesses began to detach themselves from the patronage of the once powerful generals because, "while the generals held some control over the allocation of opportunities in the Thai home market, they had much less when it came to exports."[4] In Vietnam, "political capital seems to generate declining returns as transition progresses."[5]

However, the transition is not easy. In many ways, the 1997 Asian financial crisis was triggered by the transition in several Asian countries, such as South Korea, Thailand, and Indonesia. China started its transition in the late 1970s and is still in the process after 3 decades. Japan, one of the wealthiest countries in the world, still relies heavily on the relation-based way compared to other wealthy nations.[6]

For multinational corporations doing business in the relation-based countries undergoing the transition, there are some unique challenges and difficulties to overcome. Thus it is important for international business executives to have a better understanding on the characteristics of the transition.

Characteristics of the Transition

The Danger of a Governance Vacuum

During a transition from relation-based to rule-based governance, the old relation-based way is declining, and realizing it, people and firms begin to reduce their investment in establishing new relationships and try to get as much from established relationships since the investment in them is sunk, encouraging opportunistic behaviors. At the same time, newly established public rules and laws may not be functioning well because for any law and public regulation to be effectively and efficiently enforced, there must be a stronger moral code and legal culture that respects the law and encourage self-discipline, for without such a culture, laws and regulations are nothing more than ink on paper. The combination of the decline of the relation-based way and the ineffective infancy of a rule-based system may create a governance vacuum that makes the society unstable and business activities vulnerable to organized crime. Furthermore, businesses may suffer from a worsening of bureaucracy resulting from the mushrooming of numerous independent regulatory agencies when a dictatorship collapses.[7] For example, after the fall of the dictator Suharto in Indonesia, corruption got worse because there was no one to keep a rein on the government bureaucracy to make sure that the demand for bribes by each government department was optimized so that the dictator could maximize his total bribe income and deliver the pubic goods that the briber asked for. After he was gone, there emerged many semi-independent politicians who acted like dukes controlling one segment of the government bureaucracy and demanding a much higher amount for bribes.[8]

The Tendency to Overregulate During the Transition

An intriguing phenomenon in societies undergoing rapid transition from relation-based governance to rule-based governance is that transitioning societies tend to implement and enforce more formal rules, even more than rule-based countries. Two examples from Taiwan, a society undergoing rapid transition from a relation-based to a rule-based governance environment, vividly illustrate this tendency.[9]

The first example is about the changes in Taiwan's primary and secondary education. Before Taiwan's democratization, the hiring of teachers was made by school principals. Although it used certain rules, such as requiring a degree from an accredited teacher's college, the process tended to be tainted by powerful politicians. During the democratization process (which may be viewed as an effort to transform from relation-based to rule-based governance system), reformers tried to eliminate the corruption in the teacher hiring process. In doing so, the reformers seemed to have overdone it: They essentially took the hiring power away from the principal and made the hiring solely rely on a very clearly defined, easily measured, and strictly enforced rule: a nationwide teachers test. Anyone who scored high on the test would be hired. Needless to say, the ones with highest scores may not necessarily be the best candidates for the job.

Another example is about the tenure and promotion process in universities in Taiwan. In order to eliminate corruption and political influence, the reformers instituted a point system that cumulates points based on teaching, research, and services. In so doing, they have essentially made administrators (president, provost, dean, and chairs) powerless in the process.

These two examples suggest that in the process of moving away from the traditional relation-based governance system and embracing the new rule-based way of governance, a society tends to go overboard, nullifying human authorities out of the fear that people at the top will abuse their power as in the old relation-based system.

The main reason for such an overreaction to limit authority's discretion in favor of strict formal rules is the long duration of authoritarian rule in which power has been abused for personal gains. Such abuses have left a deep indelible scar on the society and the people so that they would rather take away any discretional power from the authorities and completely rely on formal, objective rules. The lack of trust in government, public officials, or anyone in power is the fundamental cause of this overregulation.

While such measures may successfully curtail the abuse of power common in the old relation-based setting, the cost of doing so for the society and business can be quite high. The discretion of authorities to make decisions is necessary in any organization or society. Indeed, if formal rules can take care of every contingency, then officials and managers are not necessary. There must be a certain amount of trust in the people who are on power for an organization or society to run efficiently. *The challenge to societies undergoing the transition from relation-based to rule-based governance environment is how to nurture and establish public trust in general and confidence in government in particular.*

Policy and Strategic Implications of the Book

While being fully aware that each business situation is different, and the application of what we have discussed in this book has to be made by the business executive in the situation, I have tried to highlight several general points that may help both business executives and policy makers in dealing with relation-based societies and the transition from relation-based to rule-based governance.

Relying on Relationships Can Be a Double-Edged Sword

It is vital for a foreign player entering into a relation-based market to invest in establishing reliable relationships in the local market. In doing so, the foreign player should realize two caveats. First, using relations to circumvent formal rules may be illegal, even in a relation-based society. Second, when the foreign player uses relations to gain advantage in the local market, its partners and competitors also use relations to try to out-compete with it. And local partners or competitors may have stronger relationships within the power circle. In the early 1990s, McDonalds's obtained a prime location in Beijing through *guanxi*, only to find that a Hong Kong businessman, Li Ka-shing, who had a stronger *guanxi* had McDonalds' evicted for Li's real estate development project.[10]

Beware of the Governance Vacuum During the Transition

The vacuum created by the transition is especially dangerous for foreign investors and firms in a sense that as outsiders, they see new investment and business opportunities created by the newly promulgated laws and regulations and rush in to do business without realizing that the laws and regulations are routinely ignored and that the insiders see the vacuum created by the transition as an opportunity to loot.[11]

What to Do With Rigid and Many Formal Rules During the Transition?

Even in a business environment characterized by numerous stifling formal rules that make doing business difficult and costly, there are booming businesses and some firms seem to be doing well, so there must be hidden ways to get around the rules to get things done. If a new foreign firm enters such a market, the first thing to do is to get a proper introduction to the insiders in the industry and learn from them. A common error is to totally rely on financial incentives or to pay a high fee to hire the most influential local player to help you. As mentioned by a seasoned businessman we interviewed in Asia,

> It is not as simple as paying money or bribing . . . If you just offer money to someone to get his business or his help, he will look down on you and will not take it. You have to show that you are resourceful in some ways and can help him to get things that he otherwise cannot get.

A foreign player entering into a new, relation-based market must be able to bring unique competences or resources that are valued highly by the local market in order to "earn" a proper introduction and respect.

At the very least, the foreign player should try to use old relations to establish new relations. As the small world network theory stated, most strangers can be connected by no more than six existing links.[12] Quite often, the foreign firm is able to find someone in its firm that either directly or indirectly knows a local player. As we showed in chapter 2, introduction by a mutual friend in this way is more effective and may earn some instant credit rather than using a local consultant who is hired by the foreign player without any existing relationships.

Once the foreign firm becomes a new insider, it should quickly learn the hidden informal rules of the game to overcome the obstacles erected by the formal rules. At this stage, local partners or consultants are very useful in helping navigate through the maze of bureaucracy and protectionism.

The Role of Government in the Transition

The role of the government in a society undergoing the transition from relation-based to rule-based governance environment is severalfold. First, assuming that the government is actively pushing through the transition, it should effectively and efficiently deal with the opposition forces, which are the vested interest groups that have deeply entrenched positions in the relation-based system. The government must be able to design and implement incentives for them to support the transition. In other words, the government needs to use its power and resources to compensate the vested interest group so that they can part with their sunk capital in the established relations without strong resistance.

Second, the government should make great efforts to minimize the social disruption associated with the transition. A radical transition that dismantles the old relation-based way almost overnight tends to cause great social upheaval and dislocation of social groups and segments and makes the government unable to effectively and efficiently govern the society. However, there is always a tradeoff between the speed of the transition and the stability during the transition. The Russian model of transforming from communism (a relation-based system) toward a more rule-based system is characterized by a revolutionary change, or what is commonly known as the "big-bang" approach, or "shock therapy." The intent is to give the old communism a strong electrical shock to knock it out; when the society wakes up, it is capitalistic!

On the other hand, the Chinese model of transition is slow and steady, while the Communist Party keeps an absolute power, a strategy termed by the party as "feeling the stones when crossing the river."

While there is a heated debate on the pros and cons of each model with no consensus, many cannot even agree on what criteria should be used to evaluate the success of the transition. Some put political freedom above everything else, while others emphasize political stability, and there are people whose sole measure of success is economic development. However, the following facts are commonly recognized: China has had faster economic growth in the past 3 decades with greater political stability, whereas Russia has established an infant democracy with greater political freedom. Based on our Governance Environment Index score, while both are not rule-based, Russia (–4.34) is ahead of China (–5.92).

Figure 8.1 provides a map of the major types of political and economic systems in the world as well as transition paths.[13] Quadrant I includes countries that politically are nondemocratic and economically follow state central planning that bans private ownership. All the former communist countries (Soviet Union, Central and Eastern European countries, China, Vietnam, etc.) belonged to Quadrant I, but there are not many countries left there. Today, probably only North Korea and Cuba are still there. Countries in Quadrant II are the ones in which

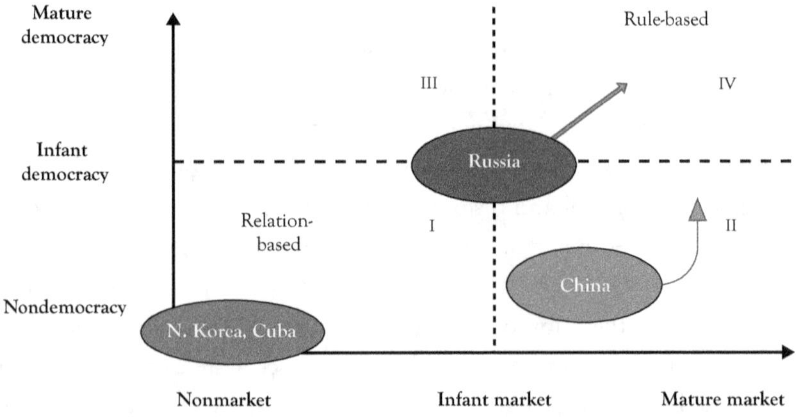

Figure 8.1. Paths of the transition: Big bang versus gradualism

the government maintains nondemocratic rule (mostly authoritarian or totalitarian) but permits private ownership and market economy, such as in China and Vietnam. There are no countries that fit Quadrant III, as mature representative democracies with checks and balances cannot ban private ownership and centralize all economic activities. The most developed, rule-based countries are in Quadrant IV, which is also the goal for most transitioning economies. The debate is not about the goal; it is about *how* to get there.

The Importance of Culture

The most daunting challenge facing a relation-based society in transition is to nurture and eventually establish a culture that is congruent with the rule-based governance system. Research shows that for a rule-based system to work effectively and efficiently, a society must firmly establish a set of norms and values that serve as a moral foundation to support the rule-based system, which must be internalized by an overwhelming majority in the society.[14] Platteau further specified that this generalized morality has to meet five conditions: (a) People internalize the value of cooperation and feel morally rewarded (in addition to economically rewarded) when they cooperate; (b) people have faith that others will follow the same moral code; (c) people cling to the code even if they have been taken advantage by defectors; (d) people feel guilty after they unintentionally have deviated from the code; and (e) people are willing to punish defectors and freeloaders. In order to establish such a generalized morality, a society first needs to nurture public trust, which, as we reviewed, tends to be low in non-rule-based societies. Second, the society must develop a legal culture that, as Platteau put it, internalizes the value of obeying public laws. A misconception about societies with a strong rule of law is that people and organizations there always resort to litigation to resolve disputes, which is costly for both the disputing parties and the society as a whole. The reality is that in highly rule-based societies, many potential disputes are avoided due to the internalization of the generalized morality, and if disputes do arise, most are mediated and settled out of court.[15]

Two Contrasting Legal Cultures

Many relation-based countries, especially the ones that have a long authoritarian tradition, have a legal culture that is the opposite of the rule-based legal culture. The essence of the rule-based legal culture is fairness and impartiality, typified in the statue of the goddess of justice, who is blindfolded and holding up a scale (Figure 8.2). The judge presiding over a trial in a rule-based society acts more like a referee in sports, whose main objective is to make sure that the two adversaries—the plaintiff and defendant—are treated equally and fairly. Both have a fair chance to present their arguments.

In authoritarian societies, especially the ones in Asia, the government assumes a paternalistic role teaching and disciplining its subjects. Contrary to the rule-based tradition that judges should be blindfolded, the authoritarian legal culture emphasizes the mission of the judge to not only take a position in the disputed case but also accurately unveil the truth and catch the perpetrator. While an exact counterpart of the goddess of justice does not exist in the Asian culture, there is a legendary judge by the name of Bao Gong in the Chinese culture, who has the superpower to read people's mind and see past events so that he has never made a single mistake in ruling. In a sharp contrast to the blindfolded goddess of justice, the legend has it that Bao Gong has three eyes—the third eye in the middle of his forehead—to help him see through people (Figure 8.2)!

Thus the main function of the legal system in authoritarian societies is to identify and punish the bad elements in a society at any cost. The judge's role is to assist the state in carrying out its political agenda by legalizing state policies and volitions. In a court, especially a criminal court, the judge takes an active, inquisitive role to interrogate the accused, making the judge almost like a prosecutor.

In the legal literature, these two traditions are called "adversarial" versus "inquisitorial."[16] In contrast to the inquisitorial approach, the adversarial way lets the two opposing parties try their best to present their evidences and logical arguments, and the rigorous cross examination tends to result in more thoroughly uncovering the facts about the case and thus having a more fair trial. This is especially true in a juried trial, which is not used in authoritarian (mostly relation-based) countries.

Figure 8.2. Images of god and goddess of justice in the East and West

Bao Gong in Chinese opera costume with a third eye, and goddess of justice in the
Western culture (drawings by author).

On the other hand, the inquisitorial approach may raise the chance of a
forced confession and a higher conviction rate in trials.[17]

Would introducing the adversarial legal culture help the relation-
based countries embrace the impartiality and fairness that are more
deeply rooted in the rule-based system? It is a reasonable conjecture.

Culture Is Hard to Change

The transformation from relation-based to rule-based governance environment is a comprehensive social change that includes different dimensions
ranging from political, economic, legal, and cultural institutions (systems).
The speed of change varies widely among different dimensions. The "hard"
(or formal) institutions, such as laws, political and economic regulations
and policies, can be changed rather quickly by government decrees, which
can be as fast as overnight in some instances. Change to culture, the "soft"
or informal institutions, usually takes a long time, sometimes several gen-
erations.[18] In this regard, government decrees do not really work—they
simply cannot order people to change the way they think.

Without the corresponding change in the legal culture, any new laws will not be effectively and efficiently implemented and enforced. Take the case of the product quality and safety problem in China that has brought worldwide attention in recent years. Ever since China became the world's factory for consumer and industrial products, harmful or illegal materials have been a problem in many products ranging from toys, animal feed, and human food, to home construction products. Perhaps the most well-known incident is the tainted-milk case, in which several Chinese dairy firms added an industrial chemical called melamine, which is used for making plastics and glues, to make the milk appear it contained more protein in lab tests, thus cutting the production cost. The additive severely affected human kidneys and caused more than 51,900 children to be hospitalized and six deaths due to kidney failure. Worldwide, numerous products in many countries were contaminated by melamine originated in China.[19]

When the tainted-milk news broke, people were outraged. People inside and outside China asked how such a practice could have existed for years and how could we prevent it from happening in the future. The culture-change perspective may provide an answer.

A brief review of China's business ethics history will tell us that this is not surprising at all. This is a product of the culture of Mao and Deng, the two most prominent figures that define China today.[20]

Mao Zedong ruled China from 1949 to 1976. His China was characterized by its extreme radical communism and absolute poverty. Being rich was shameful, Mao told his subjects. The less property one had, the more glorious one became. Private property was not respected or protected. In order to achieve our revolutionary goals, we must break the laws, the Great Helmsman taught the masses. Mao proudly called himself "lawless." The net result: little respect for property rights, and the end justifies any means.

Mao's death in 1976 brought an end to his ultraleftist ruling. Beginning in 1978, China began its "reform." Deng Xiaoping, who ruled for the next 20 years, was a pragmatic man with a vision of making China prosperous. One of his most famous sayings was a 180-degree reversal from Mao: "Getting rich is glorious." The Chinese people took him seriously. They began to get rich. But neither Deng nor his successors realized that to emulate the success of the advanced economies, China needs not only written laws that protect property rights but also a culture that encourages trust and honesty. Needless to say, neither Deng nor his successors have had any success in nurturing such a business culture.

Thus the combination of Mao's lawless legacy and Deng's call for "getting rich" has mutated into a unique capitalism with Chinese characteristics in which people can get rich by any means—even if it means to cut corners in product quality or use poisonous additives. Thus we observe simultaneously the booming of moneymaking activities and the poisonous baby formula in China.

Will China's capitalism ever evolve into a stage in which we can fully trust the safety of its products (i.e., a more rule-based stage)? No doubt the Chinese government is making a great effort to reduce fake and problem products by promulgating many laws and punishing many corrupt officials. However, as we just discussed, while laws can be made overnight, culture changes slowly. Mao's influence on Chinese business culture and practice will be there for a long time. As long as the CEOs of dairy product companies in China can sleep soundly knowing that their products are killing babies, the practice will continue. Under the combination of Mao and Deng, the world should be prepared to see more fake and unsafe products from China.

The Puzzles Solved: Together or Separate Checks?

In their book on the Chinese style of communication, Gao and Ting-Toomey provided the following observation: The Chinese way of communication "can create enormous difficulty for Chinese in interactions with strangers (outsiders) because most Chinese do not feel comfortable or knowledgeable about dealing with strangers."[21] A similar observation is made by Wallach and Metcalf in how Americans perceive the Asians' attitude and behavior:

They [Americans] interact with Asians socially as well as at work and find them to be among the kindest, most considerate, and polite people they have ever met. Then, they meet other Asians in a public situation (on a bus, driving in traffic, in the market) and see them as rude, impolite, and inconsiderate. They wonder how people from the same culture can behave so differently.[22]

Wallach and Metcalf's observation is similar to one of the puzzles we posed in the introduction—why Americans greet strangers on the street and the Chinese don't.

While these observations are quite accurate and even insightful, they do not explain what the root cause for such attitude and behavior is. With our analysis of rule-based versus relation-based systems, it is now clear that a major cause for of Chinese clearly distinguishing "insiders" from "outsiders" is that *in a relation-based governance environment, people do not need to deal with strangers.*

What is behind the culture of excluding and thus ignoring strangers is the political and economic institutions that forced people and firms to rely on other people and firms with whom they have a close relationship to overcome the "institutional holes" in the legal system. When the state cannot enforce public rules impartially, people invest in private relationships and rely on them for protection.

Coming back to the puzzle why Chinese compete to pay for group meals while Americans ask for separate checks, we can now explain it with a clear logic: In a relation-based society, people tend to deal only with people they know very well. They have close ties and interact on a frequent basis. It is feasible that every member of the close-knit group takes turns to pay for the group meal rather than calculating each member's share every time. But more importantly, it creates a familial, altogether warm feeling within the group. It is a bonding effort (or "team building," in modern management jargon). What if there is someone who always evades to pay? In a small group with repeated interaction, a freeloader will be kicked out of the group. In a relation-based society, being shunned by a group is a signal that someone is not a good prospect for business or any partnership, which is essentially a death sentence as far as this person's career is concerned. So any rational person will avoid such a perception at any cost. And this is why the relation-based culture holds loyalty, honor, and reciprocity as paramount in its value system.

In contrast, in a rule-based environment, it is expected that people deal with strangers all the time, in one's business or social life. If one has lunches with different people frequently, including people one is introduced to for the first time and may never see again, then it would be easier to "go Dutch" so that there is no obligation to pay back with another meal or unfulfilled reciprocity.

What Can We Learn From the Relation-Based Way?

From the perspective of the rule of law, using the relation-based way to obtain public goods and services controlled by the government is illegal. It usually involves bribing the official in power to get the goods or services one otherwise cannot get through legal channels. (Of course, it can be argued that the reason one circumvents the legal channel to obtain the public goods illegally through private relations is that the legal way of distributing the goods and services is not fair, and the government is monopolizing too many resources at the cost of social equity and efficiency.) As a general principle, we are not encouraging people and firms to break the law, even if the law is not fair.

The Advantage of Relation-Based Interfirm Collaboration

In chapter 1, we explained that in contract fulfillment and enforcement, the relation-based way can be more complete than the rule-based way because the latter can only fulfill and enforce what is written, whereas the former can go beyond it and follow the mutual feeling and the common spirit between two parties. This is an advantage of the relation-based way of doing business.

In a research on the interfirm relationship in Vietnam, the authors used cases to illustrate this point very convincingly.[23] In one case, a manager of a subcontracting firm located in a remote place asked the manager of the client firm for help to deal with government bureaucracy (because the client was in the capital city and was more experienced) on an order unrelated to the client firm. The manager at the client firm analyzed the order and pointed out that it was not efficient for the subcontractor to do it in-house and helped the subcontractor to outsource it. In another example, a contractor received an export order unrelated to the client. But the contractor did not have the export license, which the client had. To help the contractor, the client purchased the order at cost and handled the export process on the contractor's behalf.[24]

Certainly, those mutual assistances were not in their contractual relationship. In fact, it is virtually impossible to specify these kinds of situations in a written contract. This cooperation is based on the general spirit of long-term collaboration and mutual help without calculating financial gains or losses each time, but in the long run, both partners benefit from the savings in transaction costs.[25]

Making Nonfamily Business Family Business

From a business operation perspective, there is much to discover and learn from the relation-based way. Guo Fansheng, the successful entrepreneur in China whom we quoted earlier in the book, is an enthusiast of relation-based management, which he calls "*qin-qing*" management. *Qin-qing* is the Chinese phrase for the affection, emotion, and love that exist among family members, which can be roughly translated into "family feeling." He strongly believes that the best way to manage an enterprise is to run it like a family using the "family feeling" management style, which, if used artfully, can make employees view the firm as their own family and wholeheartedly put their maximum effort into their work. So instead of repudiating family business as old-fashioned, he calls for nonfamily firms to be run like a family firm.[26]

From a different perspective, economists George Akerlof and Robert Shiller have argued the same underlying theme when comparing the success of Toyota in Japan and the failure of Kaiser, a car company in Argentina. They showed that trust is one of the major factors that explains their difference in success and failure.[27] From the perspective of our discussion, Japan is traditionally a relation-based society with a high level of trust, whereas the trust level in Argentina is low (see chapter 2). The relation-based way has enabled Toyota to build close working relationships between managers and workers and be run more like a family business.

How can such an organizational culture be nurtured in large corporations, especially in a rule-based environment where most transactions are kept at an arm's length and where work and family are more clearly demarcated? In this book, we have been arguing that the "family feeling" style (the relation-based way) is only practical when an organization is small. How can the CEO of a large company give personal treatment to thousands of employees?

While this is a new subject that needs to be studied, here are some preliminary observations that may give us some ideas. Guo has the following advice based on his experience. When his firm was small and private, he would approve a company loan for his managers when they wanted to buy a house. That was OK, Guo said, since the company was his and he treated his managers as family members. When his firm grew big and received outside investment, it became inappropriate for him to dole out company loans to his managers. So in order to preserve the family feeling among his senior managers, he loaned his personal money to a senior manager to buy a house. "When your company grew big, you must institutionalize the family feeling. To do it, you have to cough up your own money; you can't use the company's money any more," advised Guo.[28] This is quite an extreme case. But the point is clearly made.

The second piece of advice Guo gave was that in order to institutionalize the family feeling in the company when it becomes big, the founder(s) must make a clear policy that bars family members from working in the company. "In order to make all nonfamily members feel that you [the boss] treat them like a family, you must first stop giving favors to your own family," Guo explained.[29]

To create the "family feeling," companies should consider giving more in-kind benefits rather than simple cash compensation. They also should offer more family-friendly and family-style activities. We have begun to see this trend in some successful companies in the West.

Ever since the sociologist Max Weber first proclaimed that in order to modernize, leaders of organizations must change from relying on personal charisma to following bureaucratic rules, seeking a charismatic leader for an organization has been viewed as old-fashioned and thus frowned upon.[30] Now it is time to rethink this philosophy: If rule-based firms can add more "family feeling" to their organizational culture, they will be more competitive. In this sense, it is to the firm's advantage to have a charismatic leader—someone who has the ability to earn trust, who has good interpersonal skills and is good at cultivation relations, and who is generous in his or her treatment of friends. Thus, in sum, the emphasis in relation-based culture—loyalty, generosity toward friends, reciprocity, the "family feeling"—is certainly something executives and managers in a rule-based market should begin to pay more attention to in order to stay competitive in the increasingly globalized market.

Notes

Chapter 1

1. This is a typical scene based on my extensive business experience with Chinese business people.

2. Political economy means the interplay of the political and economic forces that shape a society's overall development.

3. Przeworski, Alvarez, Cheibub, and Limongi (2000).

4. Harrison and Huntington (2000).

5. Dixit (2004).

6. Li (1999); Shaomin Li et al. (2004).

7. Phongpaichit and Baker (2000).

8. Phongpaichit and Baker (2000), p. 37.

9. Phongpaichit and Baker (2000), p. 47.

10. Siaw (1983), pp. 108–111.

11. Hiebert (1996), p. 80.

12. Kalathil and Boas (2003).

13. Li et al. (2008).

14. Hewison and Thongyou (2000), p. 209.

15. Wu (2008).

16. Bradsher (2004).

17. Phongpaichit and Baker (2000), p. 37.

18. Nguyen, Weinstein, and Meyer (2005), p. 224.

19. Ueda (2000), p. 175.

20. Li (1999); Li (2002).

Chapter 2

1. Li and Filer (2007).

2. In order to examine whether the GEI is a robust measure of rule-based governance environment, we have also conducted a clustering analysis and the result is quite similar that the countries that have a positive GEI are grouped in the same cluster characterized by strong political rights, rule of law, free flow of information, high public trust, and high-quality accounting standards.

3. Uslaner (2002).

4. Arrow (1972).

5. Li and Wu (in press); Tang (2005); World Value Survey (2005).

6. Phongpaichit and Baker (2000), p. 33.

7. Siaw (1983), p. 127.

8. Kim (2008), p. 60.

9. Nguyen, Weinstein, and Meyer (2005), p. 228.

Chapter 3

1. Xinhuashe (2006).

2. Nanfangwang (2006).

3. Hewison and Thongyou (2000), p. 213.

4. Phongpaichit and Baker (2000), p. 33.

5. Xinhuashe (2005).

6. Xinhuashe (2005).

7. Wu (2008), p. 404.

8. Wu (2008), p. 341.

9. Hiebert (1996), p. 67.

10. Kim (2008), p. 75.

11. Risk Management (2009), p. 33.

12. Phongpaichit and Baker (2000), p. 35.

13. Kim (2008), p. 77.

14. Telephone interview conducted by author with A. Watkin in Shanghai from Norfolk, VA (2009).

15. Borsuk (1999), p. 166.

16. Borsuk (1998).

17. Brown (2008).

18. Phongpaichit and Baker (2000), p. 33.

19. Phongpaichit and Baker (2000), pp. 33–38.

20. Habir (1999), p. 175.

21. Ministry of Foreign Trade and Economic Cooperation (2009).

22. Hiebert (1996), p. 68.

23. Li and Samsell (2009).

24. Li et al. (2009).

25. Personal interview conducted by author with S. Kamdar in Norfolk, VA (2004).

26. Fang (2004).

27. Bernstein (1992).

28. Diamonds.Net (2004).

29. Gemological Institute of America (GIA) (2004).

30. Diamond Administration of China (2004).

31. Bernstein (1992).

32. Personal interview conducted by author with S. Kamdar in Norfolk, VA (2004).

Chapter 4

1. Yehehua.net (2009).
2. Yang (2008).
3. Zhou (2009).
4. Chi (2008).
5. Kato and Long (2006).
6. Li et al. (2008).
7. Ueda (2000), pp. 171–176.
8. Bradsher (2004).
9. Kim (2008), p. 73.
10. Li (2005b).
11. Zhang (2002).

12. Another major factor affecting the type of foreign investment inflow is the government's regulation on the capital market. In some countries, the stock market is not completely open to foreign investors. In our analysis, we have controlled for such effect.

13. International Monetary Fund (IMF) (2003).

Chapter 5

1. Hudong (2008).
2. Hudong (2008); Wu (2008).
3. Shimoni (2008).
4. Li (2009).
5. Li, Park, and Li (2004).
6. Hiebert (1996), p. 82.

7. Personal interview conducted by author with a J. P. Morgan executive in Hong Kong (1994).

8. Kim (2008), p. 31.

9. This may sound contradictory, but it is actually consistent with what we said earlier about the role of a CEO's secretary in relation-based firms. What we mean here is that relative to the managers who are further away from the CEO, the secretary's influence tends to be greater.

10. Li and Yeh (2008).
11. Li (2009).

12. Personal Interview conducted by author with an American manager in Shenzhen, China (1999).

13. Kim (2008), p. 62.
14. Li et al. (2004).
15. Kim (2008), p. 58.
16. Telephone interview conducted by author with X. Lin, Norfolk, VA.

17. Petison and Johri (2008).

18. Petison and Johri (2008), p. 752.

19. While similar situations may also occur in more rule-based countries in select industries, it is far more prevalent and severe in relation-based societies.

20. Black and Gregersen (1999); Shankar, Ormiston, Bloch, Schaus, and Vishwanath (2008); Shay and Bruce (1997).

21. Black and Morrison (1998); Rosenzweig (1994).

22. Li and Maurer (2005).

23. Personal interview conducted by author with an American manager in Shenzhen, China (1999).

24. Li and Maurer (2005).

25. Petison and Johri (2008).

Chapter 6

1. Liang, Li, and Wu (2009).

2. Li (2005a). p. 112.

3. Kalathil and Boas (2003).

4. Kalathil and Boas (2003), p. 136.

5. Kalathil and Boas (2003), p. 136.

6. Reporters Without Borders (2005).

7. O'Brien (2007).

8. Yang (2007).

9. Reporters Without Borders (2003–2009).

10. Gao and Ting-Toomey (1998), pp. 76–77.

11. Mintzberg (1979), pp. 343–344.

12. Kim (2008), p. 31.

13. Hofstede and Hofstede (2005).

14. Guo (2008), p. 243.

Chapter 7

1. Of course, in a rampantly corrupt society, corrupt officials use their power to protect themselves, so their chance of being caught and prosecuted tends to be low.

2. Li (2004a).

3. Transparency International (2008).

4. Lui (1985).

5. However, the danger is that the bureaucrats who get the taste of the fruit of corruption will institute more stifling regulations to extort more bribes. This is why there are many examples of countries that sink into the vicious cycle where more regulations and control lead to more corruption, which makes the economy more stagnant.

6. Li and Wu (2009).

7. Li and Wu (2007).

8. Gutmann (2004), p. 124.

9. Wedeman (1997).

10. Li and Wu (2009).

Chapter 8

1. Personal interview conducted by author with P. Wang in Hong Kong (2001).

2. Li, Park, and Li (2004).

3. Huang and O'Neil-Massaro (2001).

4. Phongpaichit and Baker (2000), p. 34.

5. Kim (2008), p. 49.

6. Li (1999).

7. Shleifer and Vishny (1993).

8. Kuncoro (2009).

9. I benefited from the discussions with Dr. Kuang S. Yeh of National Sun Yat-sen University in Kaohsiung, Taiwan, during my visits from 2007 to 2009.

10. "The Ultimate Takeaway" (1994).

11. Li (1999).

12. Gurevich (1961)

13. Li et al. (2008).

14. Platteau (1994).

15. Li and Filer (2007); Li et al. (2009); Platteau (1994).

16. World Law Direct (2008).

17. Insideprison.com (2006).

18. North (1990).

19. World Health Organization (WHO) (2008).

20. Li (2004b).

21. Gao and Ting-Toomey (1998), p. 49.

22. Wallach and Metcalf (1995), p. 161.

23. Nguyen, Weinstein, and Meyer (2005).

24. Nguyen, Weinstein, and Meyer (2005), p. 226.

25. While this kind of cooperation also exists in rule-based countries, it is more prevalent in relation-based countries.

26. Guo (2008).

27. Akerlof and Shiller (2009).

28. Akerlof and Shiller (2009), p. 262.

29. Akerlof and Shiller (2009), p. 263

30. Weber (1904–1905; 1958).

References

Akerlof, G. A., & Shiller, R. J. (2009). *Animal spirits: How human psychology drives the economy, and why it matters for global capitalism.* Princeton, NJ: Princeton University Press.

Arrow, K. (1972). Gifts and exchanges. *Philosophy and Public Affairs, 1,* 343–362.

Bernstein, L. (1992). Opting out of the legal system: Extralegal contractual relations in the diamond industry. *Journal of Legal Studies, 21,* 115–157.

Black, J. S., & Gregersen, H. B. (1999, March–April). The right way to manage expatriates. *Harvard Business Review,* 52–63.

Black, J. S., & Morrison, J. (1998). *HCM beverage company.* Richard Ivey School of Business Case, University of Western Ontario, London, Ontario, Canada.

Borsuk, R. (1998, December 30). The Suharto regime blew many chances to amass wealth. *Wall Street Journal,* p. 1.

Borsuk, R. (1999). Markets: The limits of reform. In D. K. Emmerson (Ed.), *Indonesia beyond Suharto* (pp. 136–167). Armonk, NY: M. E. Sharpe.

Bradsher, K. (2004, November 9). Informal lenders in China pose risks to banking system. *New York Times,* p. 1.

Brown, P. J. (2008). US twist to Thaksin court case. *Asian Times.* Retrieved August 2, 2008, from http://www.atimes.com/atimes/Southeast_Asia/JH02Ae01.html

Chi, Y. (2008). *Chinese Communist Party promotes space walk, netizens: Can't save the party.* Retrieved July 15, 2009, from http://www.theepochtimes.com

Diamond Administration of China. (2004). *Government agencies and trade guide.* Retrieved September 16, 2004, from http://www.sdea.gov.cn

Diamonds.Net. (2004). *Rapaport diamond report.* Retrieved September 20, 2004, from http://www.diamonds.net/

Dixit, A. (2004). *Lawlessness and economics: Alternative modes of governance.* Princeton, NJ: Princeton University Press.

Gao, G., & Ting-Toomey, S. (1998). *Communicating effectively with the Chinese.* Thousand Oaks, CA: Sage.

Gemological Institute of America (GIA). (2004). *What is GIA? Retrieved September 16,* 2004, from http://gia4cs.gia.edu/cm/about-gia/mission-story.htm

Guo, F. (2008). *The China model: Guide for family business growth.* Beijing: Peking University Press.

Gurevich, M. (1961). *The social structure of acquaintanceship networks.* Cambridge, MA: MIT Press.

Gutmann, E. (2004). *Losing the new China: A story of American commerce, desire and betrayal.* San Francisco: Encounter Books.

Gwartney, J., & Lawson, R. (2002). *Economic freedom of the world: 2002 annual report.* Toronto: The Fraser Institute.

Habir, A. D. (1999). Conglomerates: All in the family? In D. K. Emmerson (Ed.), *Indonesia beyond Suharto: Polity, economy, society, transition* (pp. 168–204). Armonk, NY: M. E. Sharpe.

Harrison, L. E., & Huntington, S. P. (Eds.). (2000). *Culture matters: How values shape human progress.* New York: Basic Books.

Hewison, K., & Thongyou, M. (2000). Developing provincial capitalism: A profile of the economic and political roles of a new generation in Khon Kaen, Thailand. In R. McVey (Ed.), *Money and power in provincial Thailand* (pp. 195–220). Honolulu: Hawaii University Press.

Hiebert, M. (1996). *Chasing the tigers: A portrait of the new Vietnam.* New York: Kodansha International.

Hofstede, G., & Hofstede, G. J. (2005). *Cultures and organizations: Software of the mind.* New York: McGraw-Hill.

Huang, Y., & O'Neil-Massaro, K. J. (2001). *Korea first bank (a) and (b).* Harvard Business School Case, Harvard Business School, Cambridge, MA.

Hudong. (2008, August 6). Daqiuzhuang. Hudong. Retrieved May 2, 2009, from http://www.hudong.com/wiki/

Insideprison.com. (2006, June). *False imprisonment in the adversarial-inquisitorial system debate.* Retrieved July 24, 2009, from http://www.insideprison.com/false_imprisonment.asp

International Monetary Fund (IMF). (2003). *International financial statistics.* Washington, DC: Author.

Kalathil, S., & Boas, T. (2003). *Open networks, closed regimes: The impact of the Internet on authoritarian rule.* Washington, DC: Carnegie Endowment for International Peace.

Kato, T., & Long, C. (2006). Executive compensation, firm performance, and corporate governance in China: Evidence from firms listed in the Shanghai and Shenzhen stock exchanges. *Economic Development and Cultural Change, 54*(4), 945–974.

Kim, A. M. (2008). *Learning to be capitalists.* Oxford: Oxford University Press.

Kuncoro, A. (2009). *Corruption inc.* Retrieved July 25, 2009, from http://www.insideindonesia.org/content/view/1082/47

Li, S. (1999, January). *Relation-based versus rule-based governance: An explanation of the East Asian miracle and Asian crisis.* Paper presented at the American Economic Association annual meeting, New York.

Li, S. (2002). Does East love guanxi more than West? The evolution of relation-based governance: Contemporary and historical evidences. *Global Economic Review, 31*(1), 1–11.

Li, S. (2004a). Can China learn from Hong Kong's experience in fighting corruption? *Global Economic Review, 33*(1), 1–9.

Li, S. (2004b). Why is property right protection lacking in China? An institutional explanation. *California Management Review, 46*(3), 100–115.

Li, S. (2005a). The impact of information and communication technology on relation-based governance system. *Journal of Information Technology for Development, 11*(2), 105–122.

Li, S. (2005b). Why a poor governance environment does not deter foreign direct investment: The case of China and its implications for investment protection. *Business Horizons, 48*, 297–302.

Li, S. (2009). *Survey of it governance and management in China and U.S.* Norfolk: Old Dominion University.

Li, S., & Filer, L. (2007). The effects of the governance environment on the choice of investment mode and the strategic implications. *Journal of World Business, 42*(1), 80–98.

Li, S., Karande, K., & Zhou, D. (in press). The effect of the governance environment on marketing channel behaviors: The diamond industries in the U.S., China, and Hong Kong. *Journal of Business Ethics.*

Li, S., & Maurer, S. (2005). Managing in a relation-based environment: A teaching addenda for international business. In J. McIntyre & I. Alon (Eds.), *Business and management education in China: Transition, pedagogy and training.* Singapore: World Scientific.

Li, S., Park, S. H., & Li, S. (2004). The great leap forward: The transition from relation-based governance to rule-based governance. *Organizational Dynamics, 33*(1), 63–78.

Li, S., & Samsell, D. (2009). Why some countries trade more than others: The effect of the governance environment on trade flows. *Corporate Governance: An International Review, 17*(1), 47–61.

Li, S., Selover, D., & Stein, M. (2008, May 17–18). *The institutional origins of profit manipulation during China's economic transition.* Paper presented at the International Conference of Corporate Governance and Financial Integration, Taipei, Taiwan.

Li, S., & Wu, J. (2007, April). Why China thrives despite corruption. *Far Eastern Economic Review*, 24–28.

Li, S., & Wu, J. (in press). Why some countries thrive despite corruption: The role of trust in the corruption-efficiency relationship. *Review of International Political Economy.*

Li, S., & Yeh, K. (2008, December). Mao's pervasive influence on Chinese CEOs. *Harvard Business Review*, 62–63.

Li, S., Yeh, K., & Bi, Z. (2008). *Business environment and management in contemporary China.* Taipei: Qiancheng.

Liang, T. P., Li, S., & Wu, S. P. J. (2009, May 16). *The effect of national governance environment on firm it governance and performance.* Paper presented at the Frontier in IT Research, National Sun Yat-Sen University, Kaohsiung, Taiwan.

Lui, F. (1985). An equilibrium queuing model of bribery. *Journal of Political Economy, 93*(4), 760–781.

Maurer, S., & Li, S. (2006). Understanding expatriate manager performance: Effects of governance environments on work relationships in relation-based economies. *Human Resource Management Review, 16*, 29–46.

Ministry of Foreign Trade and Economic Cooperation. (2009). Official Web site of the Ministry of Foreign Trade and Economic Cooperation. Retrieved July 20, 2009, from http://www.cofortune.com.cn/moftec_cn/index.html

Mintzberg, H. (1979). *The structure of organizations.* New York: Prentice Hall.

Nanfangwang. (2006). *Five monopolistic industries account for 80% of new profits, encroaching other industries.* Retrieved July 30, 2009, from http://news.xinhuanet.com/english

Nguyen, T., Weinstein, M., & Meyer, A. D. (2005). Development of trust: A study of interfirm relationships in Vietnam. *Asia Pacific Journal of Management, 22*, 211–235.

North, D. (1990). *Institutions, institutional change, and economic performance.* Cambridge: Cambridge University Press.

O'Brien, L. (2007). *Yahoo betrayed my husband.* Retrieved September 22, 2008, from http://www.wired.com/politics/onlinerights/news/2007/03/72972

Petison, P., & Johri, L. M. (2008). Dynamics of the manufacturer-supplier relationships in emerging markets: A case of Thailand. *Asia Pacific Journal of Marketing and Logistics, 20*(1), 76–96.

Phongpaichit, P., & Baker, C. (2000). Chao Sua, Chao Pho, Chao Thi: Lords of Thailand's transition. In R. McVey (Ed.), *Money and power in provincial Thailand* (pp. 30–52). Honolulu: University of Hawaii Press.

Platteau, J. (1994). Behind the market stage where real societies exist: The rule of public and private order institutions. *Journal of Development Studies, 30*(3), 533–577, 753–817.

Przeworski, A., Alvarez, M., Cheibub, J., & Limongi, F. (2000). *Democracy and development: Political institutions and well-being in the world, 1950–1990.* Cambridge: Cambridge University Press.

Reporters Without Borders. (2003–2009). *Press freedom index.* Retrieved July 22, 2009, from http//:www.rsf.org

Reporters Without Borders. (2005, September 6). *Information supplied by Yahoo! helped journalist Shi Tao get 10 years in prison*. Retrieved September 20, 2009, from http://www.rsf.org/Information-supplied-by-Yahoo.html

Risk Management. (2009, April). International profile: Indonesia. *Risk Management, 32*–33.

Rosenzweig, P. M. (1994). *Colgate-Palmolive managing international careers*. Harvard Business School Case, Harvard Business School, Cambridge, MA.

Shankar, S., Ormiston, C., Bloch, N., Schaus, R., & Vishwanath, V. (2008, Spring). How to win in emerging markets. *MIT Sloan Management Review*, 19–23.

Shay, J., & Bruce, T. J. (1997, February). Expatriate managers. *Cornell Hotel & Restaurant Administration Quarterly, 30*–40.

Shimoni, B. (2008). Separation, emulation, and competition: Hybridization of styles of management cultures in Thailand, Mexico, and Israel. *Journal of Organizational Change Management, 21*(1), 107–199.

Shleifer, A., & Vishny, R. (1993). Corruption. *Quarterly Journal of Economics, 108*(3), 599–617.

Siaw, L. K. L. (1983). *Chinese society in rural Malaysia*. Oxford: Oxford University Press.

Tang, W. (2005). *Public opinion and political change in China*. Palo Alto, CA: Stanford University Press.

Transparency International. (2008). *Corruption perception index*. Retrieved July 30, 2009, from http://www.transparency.org

Ueda, Y. (2000). The entrepreneurs of Khorat. In R. McVey (Ed.), *Money and power in provincial Thailand* (pp. 154–194). Honolulu: Hawaii University Press.

The ultimate takeaway. (1994, November. 26). *The Economist, 333*(7891), 36.

Uslaner, E. M. (2002). *The moral foundations of trust*. Cambridge: Cambridge University Press.

Wallach, J., & Metcalf, G. (1995). *A practical guide for Asians on how to succeed with U.S. managers*. Singapore: McGraw-Hill.

Weber, M. (1958). *The protestant ethics and the spirit of capitalism*. New York: Charles Scribner's Sons.

Wedeman, A. (1997). Looters, rent-scrapers, and dividend-collectors: Corruption and growth in Zaire, South Korea, and the Philippines. *Journal of Developing Areas, 31*(4), 457–478.

World Health Organization (WHO). (2008). *Melamine-contamination event, China, 2008*. Retrieved March 22, 2009, from http://www.who.int/foodsafety/fs _management/infosan_events/en/index.html

World Bank. (2000). *World development indicators*. Washington, DC: Author.

World Law Direct. (2008). *Adversarial system vs. inquisitorial system.* World Law Direct. Retrieved July 13, 2009, from http://www.worldlawdirect.com/forum/civil-litigation/14409-adversarial-system-vs-inquisitorial-system.html

World Value Survey. (2005). World value survey. World Value Survey Association. Retrieved April 20, 2009, from http://www.worldvaluessurvey.org/

Wu, X. (2008). *China: The era of grabbing wealth: Business history, 1993–2008.* Taipei: Yuanliu.

Xinhuashe (New China News Agency). (2005). *The Chinese state allows private capital entering controlled industries.* Retrieved June 22, 2009, from http://www.politeian.org/spiritcn/bbs/viewthread.php?tid=6662

Xinhuashe (New China News Agency). (2006). *Our government will maintain absolute control over seven major industries.* Retrieved June 22, 2009, from http://www.cenn.cn/Info/NewsShow/ShowNews.Asp?newsid=28121

Yang, J. (2007, November 6). *Testimony before the committee on foreign affairs, U.S. House of Representatives, Committee on Foreign Affairs.* Washington, DC. Retrieved November 6, 2008, from http://blog.wired.com/27bstroke6/files/testimony_yang.pdf

Yang, J. (2008). *Tombstone: Documenting China's great famine in the 1960s.* Hong Kong: Cosmos Books (Tian-di).

Yehehua.net. (2009, February 20). *Father's stories about the Cultural Revolution.* Retrieved September 19, 2009, from http://yehehua.net/weblog/archives/330

Zhang, W. (2002, October 18). What is behind the disputes over the ownership of tiange technology? *China Economic Times.* Retrieved September 22, 2004, from http://finance.sina.com.cn/t/20021018/1027268300.html

Zhou, S. (2009). *Chinese Communist Party doctors photo, erasing "republic of China."* Retrieved June 23, 2009, from http://www.epochtimes.com/b5/9/3/11/n2458472.htm

Index

Note: The italicized *f*, *t*, and *a* following page numbers refer to figures, tables, and appendix, respectively.

A
accounting standard, quality of, 19, 20, 22, 30
adversarial approach, 120
Akerlof, George, 126
Argentina, 21*t*, 28*t*, 29*t*, 99*t*, 126
Arrow, Kenneth, 23
Asian financial crisis, 113

B
Bao Gong, 120, 121
Benidicto, Robert, 108
Bernstein, Lisa, 46, 49
big bang versus gradualism, 118*f*
Boas, T., 87
bribe, 7, 14, 37, 39, 77, 95, 96, 102–4, 106–9, 114
business groups in relation-based markets, 40

C
Callahan, Michael, 87
channel exclusivity, 47
China, 1, 2, 4, 8–10, 21, 24, 25, 29, 33–38, 42, 44, 46–50, 53
corruption, 104–7, 104*t*
China International Trust and Investment Corp (CITIC), 111–12
Chinese Communist Party, 54, 58, 105
clustering of more relation-based versus more family-based countries, 28*t*
commitment problem, 92–93
communication
downward, 92
high-context, 88, 89, 92
low-context, 88, 92
upward, 91, 92
Conjuangco, Manuel, 107
corporate governance effect, 93–94
corruption
bad effect on society, 95–96
China, 104–7, 104*t*
economic efficiency and, 100
economic growth and, 101*f*
governance environment and, 97–100
income and, 101*f*
Philippines, 104, 104*t*, 107–8
relation-based societies, 95–109
trust and, 102–4
worldwide, 96–97
Corruption Perception Index (CPI), 97, 97*f*, 98*t*–99*t*, 101*t*, 104*t*
cost, relation-based governance system, 11–16, 13*f*, 15*t*
culture
change and, 121–23
compatibility, 88–89
importance, 119

D
data sources of calculating GEI, 30*a*
data used to measure types of trust, 31*a*
De Beers, 46
decision mode compatibility, 90–91
Deng Xiaoping, 68, 105, 122–23
diamonds
barriers to entry, 46–47
market in United States and China, 46–51
digitization, 83, 84

differences
    between rule-based and relation-
        based governance, 15*t*
    in working relationships between
        two environments, 75–78
direct investment, 59–60
disclosed information, 53–63
Disini, Herminio, 108
dispute resolutions, 49–50
distributions of return on assets in
        China, United States, and nor-
        mal distribution, 57*f*

E
earnings management in relation-
        based societies, 53–54
East Asian economic miracle, 2–5
economic efficiency, 100
economic growth, 101*f*
entry barriers
    diamond, 46–47
    high market, 37–38
ex ante monitoring, 9, 13, 24, 25, 57
exit barriers, 39
expatriate
    failure, 73–75
    performance, 78
ex post monitoring, 9, 10, 13, 24, 25,
        58

F
family-based governance, 27
family business, 126–27
family feeling, 126–27
Feng Lun, 34
foreign investment flows, 58–59
formal rules
    in relation-based organizations,
        69
    in relation-based societies, 35–37
free flow of information, 86*f*

G
Gao, G., 88, 123
Gemological Institute of America
        (GIA), 47
god and goddess of justice, 121*f*
governance

and corruption, 97–100
cost of relation-based systems, 13*f*
cost of rule-based systems, 13*f*
and economic systems, 15*t*
environment, 97–100
environment and foreign invest-
        ment, 62*f*
mode, 60–64
vacuum, 113, 116
Governance Environment Index
        (GEI), 19–22, 27, 30*t*, 45, 62,
        62*f*, 97*f*, 100
    by country, 21*t*
government
    and business, 33–35
    in transition, 117–19
greatest leap forward, 111–27
guanxi culture, 25, 105, 116
Guo, Fansheng, 92–93, 126, 127

H
high market
    entry barrier, 37–38
    exit barrier, 39
Hofstede, G., 92
Huang Mengfu, 35
human resource management prac-
        tices, 71

I
income and corruption level, 101*f*
indirect investment, 59–60
Indonesia, 3, 21, 28, 29, 36, 38–40,
        76, 80, 98*t*, 113
informational compatibility, 90
information and communications
        technology (ICT)
    cost, 85*f*
    effect on corporate governance,
        93–94
    use and efficiency, 84–85
information goods, 83–85
information management
    by firms, 55–56
    by relation-based government, 54–55
information sources, diamonds,
        47–48
information technology (IT), 83

innovation lack in relation-based
    societies, 41
inquisitorial approach, 120
interface between governance and
    ICT, 88–94
interfirm collaboration, 125–26
interim monitoring, 9–10
Internet and relation-based societies,
    85–88, 86*f*
investment
    protection in relation-based mar-
        kets, 53–63
    type, 60–64
    in working relationships, 76–77

J
jobs scope, 75

K
Kaiser, 126
Kalathil, S., 87
Kato, T., 56
Kim, Annette, 70

L
Lantos, Tom, 87
legal cultures, 120–21
Li, Shuhe, 5
Li Ka-shing, 116
Long, C., 56

M
Malaysia, 8, 21*t*, 25, 28*t*, 29*t*, 99*t*
management information system
    (MIS), 90
management and working relation-
    ships, 65–81
managers, 65–81
Mao Zedong, 54–55, 105, 122–23
Marcos, Ferdinand, 107–8
market structure, relation-based soci-
    eties, 33–51
McKinsey, 111–12
measuring relation-based governance,
    22–26
Metcalf, G., 123–24
Mintzberg, H., 90
multinational corporation (MNC), 80

N
network
    social, 5, 8, 14, 15, 22, 25, 105,
        109
    informal, 7, 26, 90, 105
New York Diamond Dealers Club
    (DDC), 46–47
Nixon, Richard, 54
North Korea, 118

O
*Open Networks, Closed Regimes: The
    Impact of the Internet on Authoritar-
    ian Rule* (Kalathil and Boas), 87
organization chart, 66–67, 69*f*
overregulation, transition, 114–15

P
particularized trust, 22, 23
people-governing transactions, 8–11
Philippines, 3, 98*t*, 104, 104*t*, 107–8
Platteau, J., 119
policy and strategic implications, 45
political rights, 19, 20, 22, 30*a*
portfolio investment, 59–62
predatory corruption, 104
private ordering, 5, 7
private relations, 67–68
process priorities, 77
Przeworski, A., 3
public ordering, 5

Q
qin-qing, 126

R
Rapaport Diamond Report, 47
relation-based countries, 19–31
    financing, 57–58
    interfirm collaboration, 125–26
    learn from, 125
    ranking, 29*t*
relation-based governance
    differences between rule-based and,
        15*t*
    measuring, 22–26
    systems, 5–8
    transition from, 111–27

relation-based organizations
corruption, 95–109
interface between governance and
ICT, 88–94
relation-based organizations
(*continued*)
management and working relationships, 65–81
market structure, 33–51
people-governing transactions, 8–11
rule-based societies versus, 16–17
structure and management style, 66–73
relation-based systems, 1–17
relationships between expatriate manager and local employees, 79*f*
rule-based countries, 19–31
rule-based governance
systems, 5–8
transition from, 111–27
rule-based organizations versus
relation-based societies, 16–17
rule-based systems, 1–17
rule of law, 3, 5, 19, 20, 22, 23, 24,
30, 42, 59, 119, 125

S
Shiller, Robert, 126
Shimoni, B., 66
Shi Tao, 87
societies
corruption effect on, 95–96
that lack extended particularized
trust, 26–31
South Korea, 2, 3, 40, 112, 113
strategic planning, lack of, 70
Suharto, 3, 36, 39, 40, 113

T
Taiwan, 3, 29, 114
talent flows between rule-based and
relation-based societies, 73
terms of working relationships, 76
Thailand, 8–10, 12, 15*t*, 21*t*, 25, 28*t*,
29*t*, 34, 37, 39, 40, 57, 66, 76,
98*t*, 112, 113
Thaksin, 39, 40

Tiange Technology, 60
Ting-Toomey, S., 88, 123
Toyota, 126
trade
flows between rule-based and relation-based countries, 43–45
patterns between rule-based and
relation-based countries, 43*f*
with rule-based and relation-based
countries, 41–42
transition
characteristics, 113–15
from relation-based to rule-based
governance, 111–27
overregulation, 114–15
Transparency International (TI), 97
trust
and corruption, 102–4
and exchange policies, 49
extended particularized, 26, 27,
27*t*, 31*a*, 104, 105, 109,
generalized, 22
nuclear particularized, 26, 27*t*, 31*a*
particularized, 22, 23, 24, 26, 27*t*,
31*a*, 103, 104
public, 19, 20, 22, 30*a*, 38, 115,
119
and rule of law, 24*f*
types, 27*t*

V
vertical communications mode, 91–92
Vietnam, 8, 125

W
Wallach, J., 123–24
Weber, Max, 127
working relationships, 76
between rule-based and relation-
based workers, 78*t*
worldwide corruption, 96–97

Y
Yahoo! in China, 87–88
Yang, Jerry, 87
Yu Zuomin, 65